KAUFMAN'S HILL

John C. Hampsey

Published by Bancroft Press
Books that Enlighten
P.O. Box 65360,
Baltimore, MD 21209

410-764-1967 (fax)

www.bancroftpress.com

Cover Art: T.S. Harris
Covers: Andrea Duquette
Maps: Thom Brajkovitch
Author Photo: Eric Johnson
Interior Design: J.L. Herchenroeder

978-1-61088-153-1 *cloth*

978-1-61088-154-8 *paperback*

978-1-61088-155-5 *audio*

978-1-61088-156-2 *kindle*

978-1-61088-157-9 *eBook*

Printed in the United States.

KAUFMAN'S HILL

John C. Hampsey

To my brothers and sisters—Bernie, Jim, Mary Kay, and Barbara

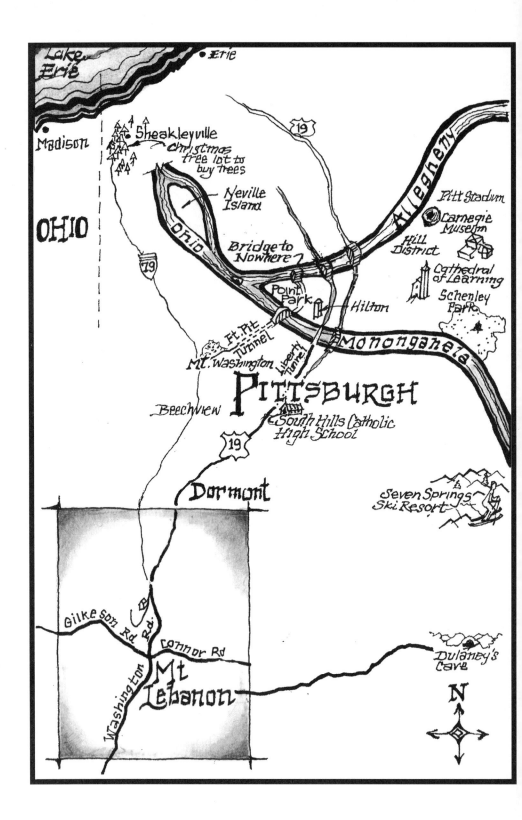

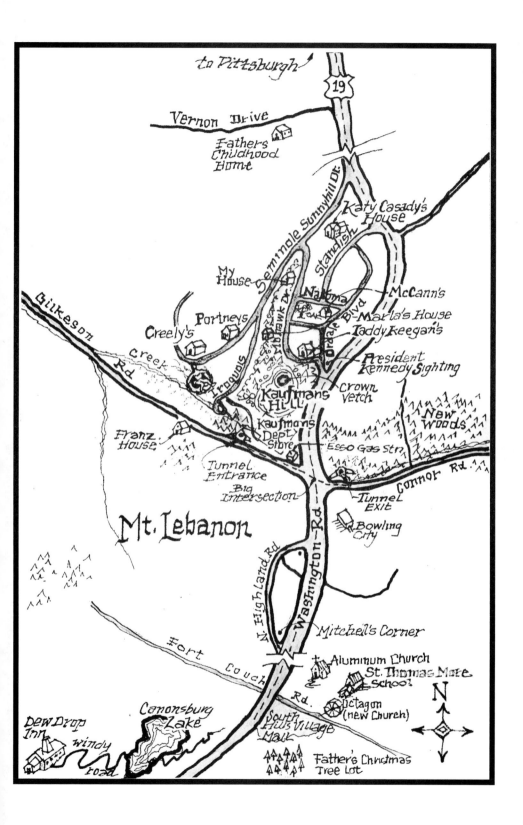

CONTENTS

Rat Stick at Twilight

I was down at the creek hitting, at just about anything, with the Creelys. We whipped our sticks at leaves and branches and rocks, and even at the soft silver mud along the creek bank.

When we got to the sewer tunnel, the Creelys stopped and balanced themselves on top of some creek rocks. The late afternoon was cloudy and smelled like rain. The air was still, except for the cool sewer dampness blowing upon us.

The Creelys stepped onto the slab beneath the tunnel and started slapping their sticks against the metal bars that crossed the top half of the entrance, until Frank Creely's stick flipped out of his hand and landed on the other side.

"Go get it," he told his younger brother.

We were all afraid of walking inside the tunnel. So Billy didn't move until Frank pushed him into the creek water. I pretended to ignore them by examining the underside of a mossy rock.

Billy ducked quickly under the bars and walked into the tunnel, his feet stretched out to the sides so he wouldn't have to touch the dark water. A few moments later, he stepped back out, holding Frank's stick in his hand like a trophy, and jumped across the creek, landing under a tree on the other side.

"Hey! Look at this!" Billy yelled.

Frank crossed the creek, his left foot and pants getting wet along the way. And I followed along the creek bank until I could see Billy poking his stick at a dead rat about the size of a small football. It was bloated in the middle, with dark matted fur and closed eyes. Billy jammed his stick at its stomach, harder and harder, until I couldn't look anymore.

"It's dead," he finally said. "What should we do with it?"

Whenever the Creelys found anything, they always thought they had to do something with it.

"Pick it up," Frank said, his voice sounding serious.

But Billy didn't move.

The air began to smell heavier, and I wished it would rain so we'd all have an excuse to go home.

"C'mon, we'll use our sticks," Frank Creely said.

I was worried, because I knew the Creelys. They might try and fling the rat at me, or knock me down and drop it on my face.

"We could take it up to the field," I said. "And bury it."

"Who wants to bury some smelly old rat?" Billy Creely said.

"You're supposed to bury a dead animal when you find it," I said.

For some reason, Frank said OK, and they followed me up the creek bank carrying the rat carefully, its dark body jammed between their sticks.

"Go on and dig a hole then," Frank commanded.

So I ran ahead up to Kaufmann's Field and chose a flat spot next to one of the big white rocks the Kaufmann's people had placed there where our woods used to be, and began scraping at the grass with the bottom of my stick. It was hard to break through the soil, though, and I was afraid the Creelys would get bored before I got anywhere. So I scraped faster, occasionally glancing back to watch them trying to balance the rat in the air. Whenever the rat fell, Frank yelled at

Billy and hit him with his stick. And Billy screamed because he didn't want the stick that had touched the rat touching him.

They continued like this, jamming their sticks harder into the rat each time, until I thought they might stab it all the way through. Eventually, they held it steady up in the air and paraded around in circles.

When I heard them whispering, I turned just in time to see their arms swing toward my face, with Billy screaming "*Aaooahh ooah-hooahh!*" like Tarzan does.

For a moment, the rat hung by its guts at the end of their sticks before soaring over my head and landing with one dead bounce on the rock behind me.

The Creelys seemed to lose interest then, and laid down on the brown grass, some of the green rat guts still hooked onto the ends of their sticks. *This is just temporary boredom*, I thought. *Eventually, they'll start up again with rat stick torture. And Frank is always the worst, because he's older and can make us do whatever he wants. Mother thinks there's something wrong with him, and that's why he doesn't have any friends his own age.*

My hole was deep but not wide enough. So I kept grinding my stick, feeling the blisters coming on as I knelt under the late afternoon light, with everything seeming to slow down. And maybe that's why I didn't hear Georgie-Porgie arrive from the direction of Kaufmann's Hill.

"What are you guys doin'?" he asked.

"Nuthin," Frank Creely said without lifting his head.

"We're waiting for him to finish digging," Billy said, sitting up on one arm.

"Why?" Georgie-Porgie asked.

"Because we're gonna bury a rat, that's why," Frank said, his voice impatient and his eyes still closed, as if he couldn't wait for Georgie-Porgie to go away.

"Well, where's the rat?" he asked politely.

"Over there," Frank mumbled, lifting his arm to point, as if he was making a great effort.

Georgie-Porgie, who was Frank's age and always dressed in adult clothes ever since his father died, stepped onto the rock and, holding his blue tie against his bright yellow shirt, examined the rat like a doctor examining an accident victim. He even touched the rat with his fingers, turning it over.

"I know just the thing to do," he said confidently. "But you'll have to wait while I run back to my house."

"We're still burying it," I said.

"Yeah. When the hole's finished, the rat's going in," Frank Creely declared.

Without lifting his head, Frank squinted his eyes at Georgie-Porgie, who glided back across Kaufmann's Field, moving pretty well for a fat kid. He didn't even seem to shift his legs as he pulled his way up through the crown vetch on Kaufmann's Hill.

At the top, his yellow shirt flicked for a moment in the light of the graying-pink sunset, and then disappeared into the woods.

I continued to work on my hole, hoping the Creelys wouldn't see I was nearly finished. *As long as they hear me digging,* I thought, *they will keep pretending they are napping . . . while Georgie-Porgie glides along the path through the woods and then runs through the backyards, his fine clothes flapping in the breeze . . . and on up Nakoma Street, toward his old brick house on Standish, where his yellow shirt finally disappears behind a screen door.*

Little Kenny Franz sat cross-legged a few feet away. Somehow, he had appeared without any of us hearing him. But Frank Creely sensed him, and stood up suddenly.

"Go pick up that rat, Kenny," he commanded.

Little Kenny stepped onto the rock and stood over the rat as if he was trying to figure a way of touching without touching. Finally, he picked up the rat by the back of its neck. And then he didn't seem afraid anymore, and even cradled the rat's body on his left arm before arranging it comfortably inside the hole.

We started burying it without Frank Creely telling us. *This will be the end of it*, I thought, *and then we can all go home*. And that's when I heard Georgie-Porgie's voice through the darkening air: "Wait! I've got something."

As he got closer, we could see a silver rod in his hand.

"This sand wedge ought to do it," he said, his body heaving out of breath. "It's the perfect club. Now, let's get everything set up . . . Where's the rat?"

"We buried it," I said.

"Here, let me show you," he said calmly.

Bending down in the dim light, Georgie-Porgie uncovered the rat and then re-covered it, this time vertically, patting the dirt firmly around the rat's neck so that only the head appeared above ground.

"So who found the rat?" he asked.

"My little brother did," Frank answered. "So what?"

"Well, he gets to use the sand wedge then."

"It was his idea to bury it," Billy said, pointing at me and looking like he wished he was already back home eating his dinner.

So Georgie-Porgie put the sand wedge in my hands, positioning me at just the right angle and setting the face of the club close behind the rat's neck.

"Don't move," he said quietly, his breath smelling like orange candy. "OK, who wants to bet he can strike it off cleanly with one swing? Any bets?"

"It's a sand wedge," Frank said angrily. "Of course he will."

"Cleanly? Do you bet a dollar? Do you actually have a dollar on you?"

"Yeah. Go ahead," Frank shrugged. "Swing the club and let's get out of here."

Everyone stood still while I tried to decide if golfing a rat's head was a bad thing to do. I thought about how my father used to play golf, and that I would probably take lessons someday. And then, in the closing dusk, the rat head got harder to see, until there was only the slice of silver at the end of the invisible club.

I wasn't afraid of hitting; I just wasn't sure I wanted to . . . and the club felt so heavy, and sickening, as I swung it back. Because I wasn't doing it right, and that's why I hit the dirt too soon.

"Give me that damn thing!" Frank yelled.

He grabbed it away and shoved me hard against the rock. I caught myself with my hand, the tiny pebbles grinding into my palm. And then I stayed like that, studying the dark outline of his body. Frank was bent over too much, not like a real golfer at all. And his swing was so quick none of us could really see it in the near-darkness. But we heard the dirt fly everywhere.

Georgie-Porgie knelt down to examine the results.

"Ha!" he exclaimed. "You've taken the top part of his body as well. You haven't done it cleanly."

He took the club from Frank, who could beat up Georgie-Porgie if he wanted to. But he was afraid. Because Georgie-Porgie was the kind of kid who never got beat up.

The Creelys sometimes kidded him, though, singing, "Georgie-Porgie, puddin' pie, kissed the girls and made them cry." When Georgie wasn't around, they changed the words to "Georgie-Porgie, puddin' pie, kissed his mom and made her cry."

"I should have known you guys couldn't do it right," Georgie-Porgie said. "Now, where's my dollar?"

"I took the head off," Frank said angrily.

"Yeah, but you took the shoulders, too. Are you going to give me the dollar, or don't you even have it? Maybe we should ask little Kenny who won."

But little Kenny was gone. He had run home the minute he

knew what we were going to do with the sand wedge.

"Forget it," Frank snorted. "Give him the dollar you have in your pocket," he said to Billy. "And let's get the hell out of here."

Georgie-Porgie took the dollar and then retreated, walking backwards toward Kaufmann's Hill.

"By the way," he hollered, after his body had faded into the darkening twilight, "it may have been the wrong club! I think a seven iron would have worked better. Ha ha, ha ha . . ."

I stayed against my rock and watched the Creelys fade into the opposite direction, their sticks high in the air as if they were still carrying the rat.

And I should have left, too, because it was late, and my mother was probably worried. But I wanted to find the rat head and bury it with the rest, even though it would be difficult in the dark.

The rain finally started falling, lightly at first. But I didn't care.

The rat head is out there somewhere, I thought. And all I have to do is touch it to find it.

But I was afraid to touch, so I couldn't move.

Seeing Him First

After Jeff Portney moved into the neighborhood, I started going to his house as a new way of escaping the Creelys. I was also hoping he'd be better than big-faced Dickie Labeau, another kid I tried playing with. Dickie would act weird all of a sudden when we were alone in my basement, screaming in a high-pitched voice and jumping up and down and spitting. He thought it was funny, but it made me nervous. And when I said, "Dickie! Please, act normal!," he only got worse.

So I stopped having Dickie over, and he started going with the Creelys, who actually liked it when Dickie went crazy. "Act like a retard!" I heard Frank Creely command one time at the bottom of the brick street. And he and Billy laughed while Dickie screamed and spit-twisted around in circles. When the Creelys got tired of it, Frank smacked Dickie a few times on the face to make him stop.

Jeff Portney lived up on the brick-street hill, near the Creelys. So when I went over to his house, I had to make sure the Creelys didn't see me. Mrs. Portney liked it when I came over. She told me I was "a nice young gentleman," and that I came from "such a nice family," which I didn't understand because Mrs. Portney had never met my mother and father. When I asked my sister about it, she said it was because our father was a downtown attorney.

Jeff was an only child, which was an "unfortunate situation" according to the neighborhood ladies. And poor Mrs. Portney, they said. Her husband always away on business. Maybe that was why she was so interested in what Jeff and I were doing. Because sometimes it seemed like Mrs. Portney actually wanted to get down on her knees and play on the carpet with us. While most mothers would be talking on the phone, or doing something in the kitchen, or staring at the TV, Mrs. Portney never seemed to do anything but drink iced tea mixed with some bottle from the cupboard and watch us. Sometimes she talked about how much she hated the Creely brothers because they had locked Jeff in her basement closet the day the Portneys moved into their new house. Then they knocked over some Atlas boxes and ran out.

Mrs. Portney complained to Mr. Creely about it, but he just laughed and said his sons were good boys and that they didn't mean anything by it. But it must have made Jeff's mother sad, even though you couldn't see it in her face because of her thick hair hanging down and her narrow body always jerking around.

Jeff and I built a "set-up" in his basement with his collection of little soldiers and cowboys. But he didn't understand that a set-up was more than just placing all the men in the middle of the floor. He didn't know they could all have their own names and live in their own places, like behind chair legs and under tables and up on windowsills, except for Christmas, when they lived in the tree.

A balsam Christmas tree lasted longer than any other, my father always said. Tinsel connected the branches like a train track they could ride along, and the icicles became silver ropes they could swing upon. Peewee, the little black cowboy man, was the best of all, because his legs were spread wide from too much time in the saddle, so he could ride down anything—branches and icicles and even the shiny ornaments. And he was so small no one could see him, which is why our cleaning lady, Lorraine, sucked him into the vacuum cleaner one day, making me cry until my mother found the little pieces inside the matted gray vacuum dust you shouldn't breathe when it floats up into your nose, and miraculously put him back together with so much brown glue that every time I looked at him I'd remember how he used to be. And how lucky I was that my father could never face taking down the balsam tree, even after New Year's; my mother making him move it to the upstairs landing where no one could see it from the street. One year my father kept it there until Washington's birthday so I had all those extra Christmas days for Peewee and my other little men in the tree, until everything seemed to drop away and death itself only existed outside the tree, which meant that any man who fell to the gray carpet couldn't come back again.

Jeff didn't know how you have to pretend to be living inside each man before placing him inside the set-up, and that's why playing with him was almost like work . . . under the fluorescent lights in the Portney basement that seemed to drift us away.

When we finished, we sat around looking at the set-up and drinking iced tea, which I wasn't old enough to drink at my house. And then we'd move things around a bit, like the white paper road that coiled across the floor, or switching some of the cowboy men from the carpet to the high ground up on the arm of the couch, or even up on the bookshelf, where they could holler warnings from above that I could almost hear. Others climbed the hill we made of mud taken from the Portney backyard, and still others swam across a lake we made from a silver bowl Mrs. Portney gave us, the lake water spilling sometimes, but she didn't seem to care.

I knew that set-ups only lasted for so long, because parents wanted their basements back again. But Mrs. Portney said her basement could stay like that forever, making me wish my mother could see it too.

The Creelys ended it . . . their invasion happening so quietly, the basement door opening without sound, and Frank and Billy and Dickie Labeau just standing there and staring. They couldn't believe the riches before them.

And then their sudden running around the Portney basement before I could even see them move, stepping on as many little soldiers and cowboys as they could, crushing the mud hill and kicking over the silver lake, with Dickie screaming and spitting, and the Creelys screaming too. Until Mrs. Portney appeared at the top of the stairs with the broom in her hands and her flowered dress flying up over her knees as she rushed downward.

"You animals!" she screamed. "Get out of here right now. You animals!"

The Creelys laughed as Mrs. Portney jabbed at them with the broom. They dodged her at first, and then they let her hit them so they could laugh even more. "There is nothing else you can do to us," their eyes seemed to say, making Jeff's mother scream, "You bastards! You bastards!," as she started swinging the broom wildly, with Frank and Billy still laughing and looking as if they were much older than eleven and eight years old.

Dickie Labeau missed it all, because his eyes were closed as he spit-twisted around, bouncing off walls and furniture, not stopping until Frank Creely punched him in the back of the neck and yanked him by the arm out the basement door.

They walked down the driveway as calmly as if they had just gotten off the school bus. When we turned back, Jeff's mother was doubled over crying in the middle of the messed-up basement floor. And that's when I left, too, running home as fast as I could, so the Creelys couldn't catch me even if they wanted to.

Next Sunday, after Mass and the Sunday breakfast my father always cooked—bacon and sunny-side up eggs inside the same iron skillet—my oldest sister asked me why I wasn't going out to play. I didn't want to tell her I was afraid of seeing the Creelys, or that I didn't want to go over to Jeff Portney's anymore, which I felt bad about.

"You'll miss seeing the president, then," she said. "Did you know he's driving by today, right along Washington Road? Around 2 p.m., on his way from West Virginia to Pittsburgh. They're going to have a big celebration downtown because Pennsylvania helped win his election. We're going to wait for him at the top of Sunnyhill. Do you want to come?"

"Maybe."

"You'll probably never get another chance to see the president," she said, before walking out the front door.

My father had told us about "the miracle of the Catholic president." But instead of going to the top of Sunnyhill, my father was at Pitt Stadium for the Steelers game. And my mother wasn't feeling well, and my other sister was over at Polly Grove's, so they wouldn't see the president waving from his convertible like he does on television. Only this time he'd be waving right past our neighborhood.

I decided to go. But instead of walking up Sunnyhill to catch my sister, I turned right onto Mohawk, figuring I could see the president sooner as he drove past the wide intersection at Ordale Boulevard.

When I got there, no one was around, except for a man in a hat standing on the other side of Washington Road. It was hard to tell if he was waiting for the bus or waiting to see President Kennedy. Because everything felt so ordinary, the cars passing by and nothing else happening. It seemed impossible that the president could actually appear. But I continued to stand on my side of Washington Road as if I had purpose.

The man with the hat crossed the street and stood next to a telephone pole a little ways behind me. I could feel him staring at me, but I tried to focus on the sky clouding over instead. Because the president should drive by when it is sunny.

A bunch of brown leaves rattled around in the middle of the street every time a car passed. They excitedly formed a circle, and then spread back out, their brittle sound amazingly loud for just being leaves.

The man with the hat talked to me, his words arriving slowly as if they were bending around from another direction. "Are you waiting for something?" he asked.

I turned but couldn't see his face, except for his moustache. His hat was just like the kind my father wore, only tilted down low.

"Maybe."

"What's that?"

"I don't know. What are you waiting for?"

He stepped back and leaned against his telephone pole like I wasn't important anymore. So I tried to forget him.

After a while, I sat down on the curb wondering what time it was, because it had to be later than 2 p.m., when my sister said the president would drive by. I thought of walking up to Sunnyhill, where my sister was supposed to be. But if the president really did come, I wanted to see him first. So I stayed and watched the afternoon get cloudier and later, everything feeling so still. Even the passing cars seemed to be slowing down. *Maybe this is how it is*, I thought, *just before the president appears, unless my sister made the whole thing up, which made me want to talk to the man in the hat and ask him if he knew anything about President Kennedy driving by in a convertible on his way to downtown Pittsburgh.* But I didn't want to talk to the man in the hat for some reason.

The sky looked like it was getting dark too early, and then I remembered my father turning the clocks back in the morning because daylight savings was over. So Sunday afternoon would end sooner.

The man with the hat moved closer again. I could hear the scratch of his pen as he wrote something down. And I didn't like the fact he could look at me and I couldn't look at him. *Next time I will have to remember that*, I thought, and *get behind someone if I am worried about him. Because then I can watch him instead of him watching me.*

I also had to remember to listen for the president, and not just watch for him—with the sirens coming around the bend first, then the line of black cars with their headlights on even though it was still daytime, like in a funeral parade. The cars rose up the hill so slowly they seemed not to be moving, except for the small American flags fluttering at the top of their antennas.

My sister was right, I thought. *The president is coming. He's just running late.* I recognized his car because it was the only one with the roof down. And there were motorcycles on either side with their sirens on, so you couldn't hear anything else.

Under the gray-white sky, the president waved, even though I was the only one there, his four fingers pointing upward and his wife in her brown dress smiling but not waving.

The man with the hat was gone.

The president's head turned from front to side, and back to the front, like a doll's head, his eyes looking beyond, as if there were hundreds of people to see, even though there was only me. As his car made the bend, he seemed to pass through an invisible tunnel, the clouds riding along above him, without any wind.

I am really seeing the president. October 12, 1962. Eight years old. His parade car traveling from Wheeling, West Virginia, right past the edge of where I live, inside the slow-down seconds.

His body rocked slightly as he passed, and a motorcycle policeman dropped his head to spit, which he shouldn't do, because it could blow sideways and hit the president.

And then the back of his head was all I could see, and his hand waving on and on to a real crowd of people farther ahead I hadn't noticed before.

I ran up Washington Road to try and find my sister. When I reached the crowd, I heard on someone's transistor radio that three hundred thousand people were waiting for the president downtown. Because he is a good man, my father said. And I saw him all alone. Even the man with the hat wasn't there.

I turned onto Standish and continued running, because I felt happy inside and didn't want to go straight home. And then down Nakoma onto Mohawk, and along the middle of the street for a while before cutting into the backyards, running fast so the neighborhood dogs couldn't catch me, and then into the small woods at the top of Kaufmann's Hill and down the side of the hill without even tripping on the vines, and across Kaufmann's Field toward Iroquois Street, which would finally take me home.

It was definitely getting dark, because of the October clocks, so I couldn't see who they were at first, standing near the dead-end circle. And then it was too late to turn back or head up Iroquois, because the Creelys would catch me either way. So I had to stop.

Dickie Labeau was with them, and Jeff Portney too, which surprised me. Frank and Billy were doing their low talking, pretending to ignore me. But I knew they were just daring me to make a run for it.

Jeff looked as if he wished he were somewhere else. And Dickie Labeau's eyes rolled in his head like he was going to explode if someone didn't do something.

Frank and Billy continued whispering, until Dickie finally did his high-pitched scream and Frank pushed him hard to the ground.

A second later, Frank turned to me. "OK, here's what we're going to do," he said in a serious voice. "You and Portney are going to fight. And the loser has to run home crying. The winner gets to stay with us."

"What if they won't fight?" Dickie asked, standing up a few feet away from Frank Creely.

"Don't you know anything, you moron?" Frank yelled. "If they don't fight, then I'll punch both of them, which will be a lot worse than these two skinny girls going at each other."

Frank's words seemed to hang in the graying air until my body could hardly feel itself, except for the back of my legs, which ached. I wanted to sit down but knew I couldn't.

I will never escape from this, I thought, *unless I stay inside all day like Jeff's mother told us to do when we were making the set-up. Because the outside world really is the Creelys' world.*

Jeff Portney had his head down. It didn't look like he was ready to fight. And I wasn't ready either, my nose worrying me the most, because it's in the open and easy to smash. So my plan was to protect my nose. I just wished my older brother had shown me how to do that, because all I had ever seen was men fighting on TV shows—hitting each other over and over again in the face, making that smacking sound. But nothing ever seemed to happen to their noses.

Frank Creely told us to move to the grass. So we walked through the darkening air toward a small hill just above the basketball court and the creek. Before we stopped, Frank pushed us hard from behind, making my head snap backwards. I tried to catch my balance, but he pushed us again, this time right into each other, my chin slamming into Jeff's nose. He looked at me with an expression I had never seen before, as if he thought I'd banged into him on purpose. I wanted to say "sorry," but there wasn't any time, because Frank pushed us again. And that's when I knew what Jeff was already thinking—*we had to fight*. And no one would see us, because we were inside the Creely-owned darkness.

Dickie Labeau hooted, his voice circling around in the thickening air. And Jeff jumped up and down, pulling on his pants like he had to go the bathroom. Then he stopped and raised one fist.

"All right!" Frank Creely said excitedly.

I considered letting Jeff hit me. Just one smack, I thought, like on television. Because it might not be that bad, especially if he didn't hit my nose. And then the fight would be over and I could fall into the damp grass. A second later I would get up like a ghost and run home with pretend-crying, just like Frank Creely wanted. Because losing to Jeff Portney would be better than staying behind with the Creelys.

But I was too afraid for my face, and at the last second rotated my arms in circles like I had seen on a Saturday morning TV show— the boys' arms acting like propellers, and no one getting hurt.

Jeff tried to punch through me, but my arms knocked his hand away. He tried again, and almost made it to my face, because I was already getting tired. *Soon he'll be able to hit through me*, I thought. *But then I won't have to worry anymore.*

Frank Creely let out a snort, and then yelled, "C'mon, you girls! You have ten seconds to cut the crap. Nine, eight, seven, six . . ."

I closed in on Jeff with my propeller arms. But he ruined it by trying to tackle me at the waist, my fists landing on his back. He moved down to my knees and my fists pounded the top of his head until he fell sideways onto the grass and looked as if he was about to cry. But, in the darkness, it was hard to tell.

A moment later, he lifted himself off the ground without even using his legs and ran toward Iroquois Street. The Creelys didn't do anything; they just let him go. And then Dickie ran away, too, which started me laughing, and I didn't know why. *Frank Creely won't like this*, I thought. But I couldn't stop. Like when someone is tickling and you can't scream. But no one was tickling or touching.

I kept watching Frank, who didn't move. And I kept laughing, which is why I missed Billy circling to tackle me from behind. He lay on top of me and tried to grind my face into the grass. Frank got on top, too, their double weight so great my breath emptied away.

"How do you like this?" Frank asked. "This is what happens when you fight like a girl."

Another minute passed without breathing, and then they finally rolled off me. I felt so limp I couldn't move. But I should have, because Frank turned me over and sat down heavy on my stomach, pinning his knees into my thin arms, rearing up with all his weight to dig in, the pain so sharp my eyes watered out. Frank probably couldn't even see me in the dark. But I could see him, through the tilted angle of the yellow streetlight.

My skinny bones will just press away into the earth, I thought. And no one will ever know . . .

Frank wiggled his body sideways to make it worse. Then he rocked forward and backward. I closed my eyes and tried counting the seconds. But he rocked for a long time.

When he finally stopped moving, everything was quiet, except for his breath, which was close on me, and some barking dog from across Iroquois Street.

"Get off of me!" I yelled.

"Why should I?" he whispered back, the sweat from his forehead dripping on my hair and his rusty breath drifting across my face.

Everything went quiet again, and I opened my eyes to see his round head hovering above, and his spit-drip shining in the yellow light. He let it slow-hang as long as he could. Billy Creely doing it too, kneeling beside him. Both trying to see how far the spit could drip before falling away.

I closed my eyes again and sealed my lips. Their spit landed on my nose, followed by the awful slow sliding down my cheek.

Both brothers' spit smelled exactly the same—like maple syrup and rusty metal. Which was strange, because if the Creelys had pancakes for breakfast, the syrup smell should have disappeared by evening. Unless rusty metal syrup was the way Creely spit always smelled.

After a while, it didn't matter, just like it didn't matter after your arms go numb. And I was just lucky Dickie Labeau wasn't there, because he was a full-time spitter. But he probably didn't know how to slow-drip spit. So Dickie Labeau didn't matter.

Frank made sure to dig his knees into my arms one last time before getting off. Then he bent over, his oversized face looking upside-down at me.

"You can go home now, little girl."

But I just lay there, as he and his brother walked slowly away into the vague darkness. I was afraid to move, because more spit would drip down my cheeks.

Minutes passed before I suddenly jerked my head to the side and wiped my face against the wet grass, scuffing it like when something is on your shoe. Only it was my face.

... and my mother never let us use the "spit" word, because it was crude, and she hated spitting, so we had to say "expectorate" instead; just like we were never allowed to say "sweat" either, because that's what horses did, so we had to say "perspire" ... And my father always telling us to thoroughly "masticate" our food, especially at Sunday dinner, with Sunday always the saddest day, and Sunday night the worst of all, unless the president drives by, and then everything feels different inside the cloudy afternoon, until a motorcycle policeman spits when the president isn't looking and you have to scuff your face across the black grass at the Iroquois dead end, all because the clocks have been set back one hour, making night come on too soon, and that's why I couldn't see them standing there in the twilight ... My father making his way through the house so slowly, so methodically, my mother says, while the bacon cooks in the grease, sputtering, just after Mass, turning the hands of each clock carefully, making me think there will be extra time that day because everything is going backwards, instead of losing time inside the Creely darkness, which doesn't make sense, but

does help explain why the president was one hour late, because no one turned his watch back, which I didn't think of at the time . . .

. . . His head turning like a doll's head right toward me, and I was the only one there.

Taddy Keegan

Taddy Keegan stepped off the bus in front of me, the first time I remember seeing him. He stood near the bottom stair like he didn't know where he lived. Everyone else moved past him.

I stopped for a moment on the last step, and then someone jabbed me from behind, right between the shoulders, and I flew into the back of Taddy Keegan. The jabber was Big Mori. I recognized his coughing laugh.

Taddy Keegan shrugged and didn't look at me. Then he spun away, arching his feet in some kind of dance-walk. *He knows where he's going after all*, I thought, *and is only pretending to look lost.*

Big Mori wasn't finished.

"Hey kid!" he yelled. "It's Gilkeson Rules!"

But Taddy Keegan continued his dance down the Mohawk sidewalk. Big Mori, whose real name was Bob Morian, yelled louder as the bus pulled away, "Hey! I said Gilkeson Rules! Did you hear me?"

Taddy Keegan stopped and half-turned around.

"Gilkeson Rules?" he echoed in a voice sounding just like Big Mori's.

He walked back to us in a stiff-legged way, with long stick-man strides. When he got close, he mooned his face around Big Mori's head, his thin lips closed but sort of smiling. The other boys laughed. But Big Mori just stared and pushed his black-rimmed glasses up on his nose. A black band was attached to his glasses, like the kind basketball players wore, even though Big Mori didn't play basketball.

Taddy Keegan kept smiling close with his fake face. And I kept thinking Big Mori would hit him at any moment. But he didn't.

When Taddy Keegan finally spoke, his words sounded exaggerated, as if he had glue in his mouth, or he was having a hard time moving his jaw. I didn't know if he was still play acting or if he had a real problem.

"Tell me about your Gillllkesoooon Ruuuules," he said in a stretch-mouth lisping way.

"Gilkeson Rules are definitely in effect," a higher-pitched voice said from behind us.

It was Little Mori, whose real name was Dennis. "Gilkeson" was the four-lane road they lived on. Little Kenny Franz lived on Gilkeson Road, too.

"Yeah, Gilkeson Rules are definitely in effect," Big Mori repeated. "Which means that if anyone bumps into anyone else, they have to fight it out."

The Creely brothers moved excitedly. But I still thought it would be Taddy Keegan and Big Mori punching it out. Until Taddy Keegan turned to me, his face finally still, and his voice low and serious.

"OK, kid. What do you want to do?"

He sounded like a cowboy from TV. And he held his breath without puffing his cheeks, while his eyes looked beyond, as if he was dreaming into some other place. Behind him, Billy Creely and Dickie Labeau giggled. Big Mori stood perfectly still, his arms crossed in front like an Indian.

The wind gusted suddenly, and I noticed a group of birds settling into the weeping willow tree on the corner. No cars were passing, and no one else was around.

Who cares about Gilkeson Rules, I thought, *because I still don't want to hit Taddy Keegan. And I don't want to run, either, because the Creelys will see me.*

So I slapped Taddy Keegan instead—just once, hoping that it might not be as serious as hitting with a fist. His head hardly moved, but his eyes suddenly stared into me as if he were noticing me for the first time.

"Did you see that?!" Frank Creely yelled. "He slapped just like a girl!"

"Slapping doesn't count," Big Mori said, uncrossing his arms and stepping toward me.

But Taddy Keegan's cowboy voice came in-between: "Kid, I'm gonna give you five seconds to run."

I only counted for one second before running across the soggy front lawns along Mohawk, and then into the backyards of families I didn't know. It didn't matter, because I was prince of the backyards, the king of cutting through . . . And I kept on running, even though I knew Taddy Keegan wasn't chasing me. Because why would he go after a skinny kid who slapped like a girl?

He is dance-stepping his way home, I thought, *to a house I don't know. And he isn't thinking of the Creelys or Big Mori, who are just stupid kids who couldn't figure out Taddy Keegan if their lives depended on it.*

The rest of September, I avoided everyone, my mother finding a way to pick me up in her gray Rambler after school without the other kids noticing. And she never asked why. She also never asked why I stopped going out to play when I got home, instead waiting for the dusk to settle in, or for the rain to drizzle. Because I knew the Creelys and Morians would be moping their way home then. And I'd go down past Kaufmann's field and the creek, to the big intersection at Gilkeson and Washington Roads, and sit on the curb across from Bowling City and the Esso station, where no one normally sits, waiting for the garage lights to come on underneath the nearly completed Kaufmann's Department Store built right on top of where the woods used to be, and where the big kids said they used to have a tree fort that no one was allowed into, except that one time Georgie-Porgie climbed up after they had all gone home for dinner, and he said there was really nothing there except a magazine about women he wasn't supposed to see and a pile of rocks by the window. The tree fort didn't even have a roof, he said, which didn't make any sense.

I was still sitting on the curb after 6 p.m., because our dinner was later than everyone else's, so there was more time for watching the traffic stop and start, like I was some crazy kid who didn't know where he lived but who believed that sitting and watching had to count for something, as the twilight vanished and the cars slowed, and the intersection lights turned on underneath the dropping darkness.

My father would just be getting home from work, placing his gray hat on the rack inside the closet door, then heading into the kitchen to make his first bourbon highball at 6:15, and his second at 6:45, my mother serving dinner at 7:00, before he was ready, and all of us having to wait while he slowly washed his face in the powder room sink, splashing the clean water against his cheeks—because he doesn't know the meaning of the word "hurry," my mother always said, while hearing the little kids starting to play again outside, because their dinner was already over, making me want to get back outside and return to the Big Intersection where it was already too late for nine year olds to be sitting on curbs, with time always seeming different the later it is in the dark.

ʌฟ1ฟʌ

One October Sunday, I went out in the late afternoon, because it was too windy and damp for Creelys to be about, and headed for Kaufmann's Hill.

I wanted to hoist myself up the hill like Georgie-Porgie did, but the vines broke off in my hands. Crown vetch, they called it—a honeysuckle-like plant the Kaufmann's people sprayed all over the slope after carving away the ground underneath. Some of the older kids called it "crown bitch," because it was so tough to climb through.

I leaned into it, sinking my feet deeper in the wiry vines, sort of kneeling my way along, with the smell of green dampness all over me, wondering just how fat Georgie-Porgie could always glide right up the hill.

When I paused to look upward, he was there . . . with a long curved weed in his mouth that he was smoking like a cigar. He looked more like a man than a boy, with his jaw jutting and his steady face saying, "I am Taddy Keegan. No one touches me."

Through his side vision, he must have seen me. So I thought of running, but I knew I would just fall down the crown bitch hill and look ridiculous. So I froze like an animal and continued to stare at him against the stillness and the yellow-orange trees.

After a while, I shifted my legs to get more comfortable and laid my head back into the damp vines that I knew were filled with spiders. But I didn't care. Because it felt like I could take a nap right there, and forget about night coming—maybe even drop right through the crown vetch hill with Taddy Keegan's face still above my eyes, and my mind dreaming of the other side beyond the dull white sky.

"Have you ever smoked a toby?" he asked, his voice carrying close. "I'll get you one if you want."

Tilting to the side, I watched him disappear behind the crest of the hill. Then I arose, my legs feeling rested, and climbed to the top like it was nothing, and headed down the path until I found him reaching into some drooping branches loaded with hundreds of curved brown tobies. I had never noticed the toby tree before. It was very near what some of the older boys called "the old bitch's yard." But I had never seen her, so I didn't know if that was true.

Snapping one toby loose, he bit off the end before handing it to me. I placed the moistened end into my mouth, and then waited while he dug into his pockets for some matches.

When my toby didn't stay lit, he shrugged as if to say, "That always happens," and walked past me toward his rock on top of Kaufmann's Hill. I followed and sat down next to him because standing behind him didn't feel right. He handed me the matches and I successfully lit my toby, and the two of us puffed away on smoke that smelled more like burning leaves than tobacco.

Below us, Kaufmann's Field wavered yellow under the fading afternoon light, making the skinny trees and large white shale-rocks that the department store people had placed there look like fake decorations.

Somehow, though, from the top of Kaufmann's Hill everything seemed to fit together with everything else—the low dark creek bed beyond the field, Gilkeson Road above it, the slope of trees to the right where the last leaves were blowing free during the very seconds I watched them. And Iroquois Street beyond, which I couldn't see but knew was there. And beyond that, the brick-street hill where the Creelys lived, who didn't seem to matter that much anymore. When I was seven, I must have already known that, sleeping over at their house one night . . . *lying in one of the four corner beds in the boys' room trying to fall asleep without hearing or smelling anything, but still having to breathe the same air that Frank and Billy and little BriBri had already breathed, which made me feel strange inside myself, and that is why you wake up even though you never remember falling asleep, trapped in a place that is too much Creely and you can't get away until morning when the outside light will press through the broken blinds. And falling once more into sleep darkness that has noth-*

ing to do with Creelys, until hearing their breathing again, in different rhythms and underneath a light rain on the Creely roof, and thinking how the Creelys never wanted me to stay over but only asked me so they could ignore me later, with Mrs. Creely yelling "All right about it! All right about it!" whenever the boys asked for anything during dinner, and Mr. Creely moving around the table with his bald-headed face above large hands, smacking the boys in the back of the head in advance of what they hadn't even done yet . . . and that's why I couldn't wait until morning, sleeping with my clothes on and shoes in hand so I could step quietly down the stairs without hearing, past the doorway into Mrs. Creely's room, where she sleeps with eyes open, and past Mr. Creely, snoring away in his recliner chair, waiting for the images to flash bright from his TV so I could find my way to the front door, and then closing it without sound, yet still disturbing Mr. Creely, who scares me with his stop-sudden snoring. But it didn't matter, because I was already gone . . .

Smoking a toby isn't hard to do as long as you have enough matches, which we didn't. So I threw my toby away.

"Did you ever think," Taddy Keegan asked, his eyes staring straight ahead, "that you could dive off the top of this hill and fly? It might be possible. No one ever tries."

For some reason, I was afraid to look at him.

"I think about flying," I said. "If I close my eyes, I can see myself."

"I don't mean that," Taddy said impatiently.

He stood, his voice sounding more excited.

"You start like this, with your eyes definitely open. Then you let yourself go."

His hands arched over his head, as if he were preparing to dive into water instead of the crown vetch hill, the burnt-out toby still hanging from his mouth.

I knew he was kidding, but I stood up anyway, not quite knowing why, until I saw him actually let go of himself like the famous divers who drop off the cliffs in Acapulco on TV. Only I caught Taddy Keegan at the waist through his brown jacket, his mouth twisting backwards with disappointment.

"Now you'll never know how to fly," he said, looking past me.

A moment later, he got his face real close, like he had with Big Mori. I could see the freckles on the top of his forehead underneath his straw hair. And when he spoke, he sounded like an actor, not like the Taddy Keegan I had just smoked tobies with.

"My pappy says if you're going to be afraid of everything, you may as well live in the sewer."

Then he skated down the vetch hill in a way that didn't seem possible, as if his feet weren't touching the vines. Even Georgie-Porgie couldn't do that.

I decided to go down myself, reverse-crawling the bitch hill on my hands and knees as if it was a crown vetch ladder. And then I ran across the field, not stopping until I reached the creek, where he was sitting on a rock with his feet inside the water, whittling at a small piece of wood with his penknife.

I waited, but he didn't look at me. So I considered going home. *Let him have the creek to himself*, I thought. *It's getting late anyway.*

I walked along the creek bank, trying to ignore him. I could still hear him whittling, though, as I tried to stay on the stones and not get my feet wet.

After a while, I decided I really should go home and began climbing the embankment. A squirrel darted in front of me and I almost slipped. And that's when he spoke to me in his regular voice.

"We should come down here sometime after it rains. I bet the creek is huge then. We could get inner tubes from the gas station. Big truck-tire ones. And blow them up and roll them down the hill and ride them in the creek."

He stood and waded through the water as if he didn't care his sneakers and pants were getting wet, or that the fading day was feeling cooler, especially with the stream of damp sewer air blowing on us.

He tossed his whittled stick into the water as if it didn't matter and put his knife back in his pocket. Then, with magic smoothness, Taddy Keegan ducked under the bars of the sewer grate and stood inside the tunnel. Because of the falling dusk light, I could see only part of him.

"Well, I guess I'm going through now," he said, as if he were about to ride away on a bicycle.

"Hey!" I exclaimed. "No one's ever gone through there. It goes under the Big Intersection, and we don't know where it comes out. And there are rats."

"Have you even seen a rat?" he asked.

His hands held onto the bars like he was in jail; the toby was still in his mouth.

"Yeah!" I yelled back. "But it was in the creek."

I heard his feet sloshing, and then I couldn't see him anymore beyond the tunnel shadow.

"Taddy, you better come back out!" I said loudly.

It was the first time I had used his name.

Being careful not to get my feet wet, I moved toward the sewer grate, the dark water's sickening breath all over me. More than ever, I thought of going home. *But what if Taddy Keegan makes it through to somewhere else? I thought. Would he come back to tell?*

The sound of his sloshing feet faded away without an echo. Soft sounds never seem to go anywhere, unlike voices and rocks. The Creelys were always so proud of the way they could scream into the tunnel and throw rocks against the metal sides to hear their echo. But they were afraid of going in, and angry at the tunnel for being there.

This time I didn't have to worry about the Creelys, or even Taddy Keegan, who didn't care what I did. And that's why I climbed under the metal bars and rushed into the tunnel, through the damp sewer smell and dark water, not caring about getting my feet wet, like when you suddenly decide to run into Lake Erie and don't even slow down for the rocks.

"Taddy, wait up!" I called, thinking, *Taddy Keegan, Taddy Keegan, Taddy Keegan . . .*

Because I couldn't face being in the tunnel alone.

And he was there, but way inside at a place where there were vague strands of light hanging like silver strings inside the black mist, coming from a place neither of us could see. But I could make out the shape of Taddy Keegan's body and his bent head, and the silver splashing water around the back of his ankles.

He continued onward as soon as I reached him, as if he knew where he was going. And I stayed close behind, judging the distance between us by the sound of his feet in the water. I tried walking on the sides of the tunnel, then gave up and walked right through the sewer water again like Taddy Keegan.

"What about the rats?" I whispered, not knowing why I was whispering.

"We're not going to see them in the dark," he said loudly. "So we can't worry about them. Besides, I have a stick."

His voice echoed forward, giving us a sense of the tunnel to come, even though there was nothing but blackness. And he kept slapping the water with his stick, probably to make sure the rats would get out of the way. I wondered where he got the stick, because he didn't have it going in, and I kept thinking how Mr. Keegan's words were right: We were in the sewer because I was afraid to let Taddy Keegan fly off Kaufmann's Hill.

Every now and then, the vague light seemed to filter in and then fade away, like vapors you can almost see. And I wasn't sure if it was somehow coming from above, or if I was imagining it. But since we were walking through a metal tube, light couldn't be coming from the outside.

This must be what it's like, I thought, *to get lost in a place where no one finds you after you die. And stopping makes no sense, because going back could take longer than going ahead.*

I listened for the noise of automobiles, because we had to be under the Big Intersection. But I heard nothing. The tunnel seemed to be the final untouchable place where you could only go in one direction, and you can't hear the outside world because it's sealed away. A tunnel that may not even come out anywhere, but just keeps on going, into the next suburb maybe. Until a mountain stops it up somewhere and the foul air inside no longer moves, which is why the most important thing inside a tunnel is oxygen.

So Taddy Keegan and I wouldn't die from rats, I decided. And we wouldn't drown in the sewer water, either. But we could lose our breath without knowing it, as the last bit of air is absorbed into the tunnel darkness.

I realized I was shivering inside my creek-soaked shoes, and that's when I heard the dog, its shrill bark seeming to come from above. But I knew that was impossible. And there was too much tunnel behind us for any high-pitched dog to have chased us all the way.

Taddy was blocking me, so I couldn't see very well. But there was a gradual coming-on of light, which I hadn't noticed before.

Taddy said nothing; he didn't even quicken his pace. I wanted to run past him, but waited. Because Taddy Keegan had taken me through the sewer that I never could. No one else had done that. Not the Creelys or Big Mori or Georgie-Porgie . . .

And there really was a dog barking when we stepped into the dull light, with a serious-looking man holding its leash. He was positioned halfway up the hill to our left and staring as if he thought we were criminals, when all we had done was walk through the tunnel.

"Forget that guy," Taddy said, as he sat down in his wet pants to light his toby.

I didn't know he had a second pack of matches. But the matches wouldn't light because the sewer had made everything damp.

The dog kept barking in loud, nervous shrieks, making me afraid. So I closed my eyes and tried to imagine that the man and his dog were gone.

"There's a tree fort," Taddy said, "farther into these woods."

I opened my eyes to see him still trying to light his toby. Beyond were woods I had never seen before, with the creek disappearing right into the darkening trees.

"That could be our new woods!" I said excitedly.

"You always have to check out your territory, kid," Taddy said, as if he didn't hear me, his voice switching into fakeness. "That's how I found the tree fort. Then I took a shortcut home, right through this tunnel."

The man with the dog stayed in place, like his legs were posted into the side of the hill. And his dog kept barking as if we were supposed to leave.

Taddy stood and sloshed across the creek toward the man, and then turned right onto a path that headed toward the new woods. I didn't follow him because there was hardly any light left, and my feet were freezing. But I wanted to see the tree fort. *Maybe I can come back sometime*, I thought, *and find it myself.*

The dog continued to bark as I watched Taddy Keegan make his way down the path. *Maybe no one really follows Taddy Keegan all the way*, I thought.

The Creelys won't know what to do with him, and Taddy Keegan won't even know they are there. And maybe that's how I could be with the Creelys, now that I had made it through the tunnel.

I climbed up the hill, slicing between the high brown grass, right past the man with the dog, never looking at his face. At the top, I turned back to find Taddy Keegan, but he had already disappeared into the new woods.

When I turned the other way, I could see everything I knew, only from the other side—Bowling City and the Esso station and the Kaufmann's department store construction site with the two "n"s in the sign fading into one because of the evening mist, so it looked like *Kaufman's*, and I decided I liked that spelling better. Our tunnel had passed under all of that, and under the Big Intersection, too. In the heavy twilight distance, I could even see Kaufman's Hill, just beginning to fade away.

For the first time, I actually wanted the Creelys to be there. "Where are you, Creelys?!" I screamed. *Tucked inside your syrup house, I bet . . .*

I ran across Washington Road, not waiting for the light to change or caring about the tooting horns, because I had made it through the tunnel and nothing could touch me. Even the Creelys couldn't, with their ugly faces and spit.

Inside the cooling dusk light, I ran past the Kaufman's Department Store site and across Kaufman's Field, which felt like mine. I glanced down toward the creek, which was barely visible under the shadowy trees, and thought I could still see the opening of the sewer tunnel inside the closing darkness.

And it was mine, too.

The Garden and the Creek

In the winter began the visits of Little Kenny Franz. I never invited him over. He just started showing up Friday nights, after his dinner, and an hour before our dinner, which is why my father would groan as he paced with his drink and cigarette in hand, flicking the ashes impatiently into his stand-up brass ashtray.

My mother would find a way to work things out, like a game of *Bridg-it* or *Clue* with me and Little Kenny that he would continue to play on his own, against himself, while my father and mother and sister and I had a quiet dinner in the kitchen. And Little Kenny didn't mind. He seemed so happy just to be in our house.

After dinner, we'd play *Password* or *Jeopardy* with my mother, because Little Kenny liked it that way, sitting on the footstool, his back arched over, excited about the possibilities of each question, squirming just a bit as he pushed his thick glasses back up his nose with a hand that seemed unfamiliar to him. And he would chuckle at things my mother and I didn't think were funny, showing his oversized teeth that never seemed to embarrass him.

I was glad my mother played with us, because I wouldn't know what to do with Little Kenny on my own. And that's why I sometimes felt envious of my father, who could always dissolve into back-and-forth pacing whenever he wanted, calling me "son" if he actually talked to me—like, "Son, it's time to get the hot dogs" two minutes before halftime at the Pittsburgh Steeler football games, and, "Son, I guess it's time to get the tree" before driving into the Christmas Eve dark, which didn't make any sense to my mother, because "who can pick a tree out in the dark?" And I knew my father would never like any of them, since he had waited until the last minute, driving my mother crazy while she waited at home to decorate the balsam tree on Christmas Eve.

Little Kenny would leave around 10 p.m., grinning slow-mouthed as if he was ashamed as he said goodbye. And I'd rush upstairs to my parents' bedroom and reach under their heavy wooden dresser for two water balloons I'd prepared ahead of time. I'd balance them in one hand while opening the window with the other, just in time to see little Kenny walking across the front lawn on his bouncy toes.

As he reached the sidewalk, I would hurl them, and in the same second wish I hadn't. But you can never call water balloons back, with Little Kenny already turning his toothy smile up at me through the dark as if to say, "I don't know why you do this. But it's OK."

I always wanted him to run or dodge the balloons, but he never did. And when I actually managed to hit him, he still didn't seem to mind, even though he would be wet and cold during his walk back to Gilkeson Road. And that's why throwing the balloons never felt as good as I expected. But I'd still throw them again the next Friday, because it was our routine. And Little Kenny would again pretend he didn't know they were coming. Maybe he figured the balloons were a fair price to pay for an evening of games away from his home.

I never told my mother about the Kenny Franz balloons. But maybe she knew. So I never had the chance to explain why I had to treat Little Kenny in the water balloon way, even though I didn't want to.

In the early spring, I carved a vegetable garden right out of our upper backyard lawn. It was during vacation week when I took my father's shovel from the garage and started digging up pieces of weeds and grass, each chunk fighting to stay in place before I tossed it behind the peony bushes.

I turned the soil over as I had seen my father do every year in his flower beds before he planted his dahlia and gladiola bulbs, working in his garden clothes that were nothing more than a worn pair of pants from one of his old business suits, a frayed gentleman's hat, and sneakers unlike any I had seen anyone else wear except my father. They were made of blue canvas, and in the shape of office shoes, only with gray rubber soles. And they were so soft that his bony toes protruded up into the canvas tops as he walked.

I finished my digging before he came home from work, because I knew that, if he saw me, he would act like the world was coming to an end. The world always came to an end whenever anything changed at our house. Like the time my mother had me rearrange the furniture in their bedroom while he was at work, because the pieces had been in the same places for nearly twenty years. And my father acted like his whole life had been traded away. "How could she do this?" he softly yelled over and over, as he stared at the furniture as if he were trying to will it back into the old positions.

After a week, he never mentioned it again. Because the new furniture positions had already become the way it always was. And that's how I learned, at ten years old, that change had to happen while my father was at work. And that's why the borders of my garden were all finished and the newly turned soil glistening silver when my father saw it in the fading after-work light. "My God, son, what have you done?" he moaned, as if I had lit the yard on fire, when I had only just dug up a useless piece of backyard lawn.

I didn't want to cry, so I ran instead—through the line of dying poplar trees at the top of our yard and across some neighbors' back lawns, cutting through their bushes and the flower gardens where "the old bitch" lived until I reached the woods at the top of Kaufman's Hill.

After making my way down the path, I sat on Taddy Keegan's rock and stared at the darkness dropping around. But I could still see my father, his round-stomached figure standing over the graying dirt in the middle of the upper backyard, believing in his mind that if he stared long enough, everything might return to the way it was, and the grass and weeds miraculously reappear.

The planting, too, I did while my father was at work. Corn and tomatoes and green beans and lettuce, and watermelon seeds I spit out myself. I didn't think anyone knew about my garden except my mother and father. But when I heard Billy Creely's voice, I knew he was standing in our lower backyard, near the border with our neighbors, the Macbeths.

"So you're growing a garden," he said in his singsong way.

He was wearing a blue baseball cap to look more important. And I started worrying again about how much he and Frank hated me because I wouldn't let them inside my house anymore, after what had happened at Jeff Portney's.

"I'm planting a garden, too," he said quickly, looking over his shoulder as if he was afraid my mother might see him. "And I bet my corn's gonna grow taller than yours."

I didn't say anything because I wanted him to go away.

"This is bad soil here, you know. The good soil's up on the hill, where we live. And my dad's got cow manure for sure. Do you have cow manure?"

I didn't know Billy Creely was a soil expert. I only knew he wanted to beat me at everything, like basketball and stick baseball. When I started my garden, I thought it would be something that had nothing to do with Creelys.

That weekend, my mother took me to the nursery to buy cow manure, which she insisted on calling "fertilizer." *With lots of fertilizer*, I thought, *things could grow well even in the bad soil underneath my father's lawn that I never should have dug up.*

All week I worried about Billy Creely sneaking in to ruin my garden, maybe using some kind of poison from his father's garage. How else could he be so sure his corn would grow taller?

On Friday night, I pitched the pup tent that I got for Christmas in the upper backyard, and told my mother I was pretending to go camping. Then I lay awake as long as I could, smelling the chemicals in the green canvas roof and trying not to worry about the spiders that I knew were crawling around, while I waited for Billy Creely to come with his garage poison to pour all over my garden.

In the early morning, it rained so hard I had to retreat inside the house. And it continued to rain all day and through the next night, so I never had a chance to take down my tent which, by Sunday, sagged in the middle and leaned to the left as if it wanted to collapse right into my garden where all the young plants were so battered I couldn't stand to look at them anymore.

So I decided to give up worrying about the garden and Billy Creely, and to go to Taddy Keegan's house instead, even though I had never been there before. I knew he lived up on Mohawk in a three-story brick house built sideways on its own little hill, which didn't make any sense, my father said, because a house should always be parallel to the street.

After knocking, I waited for a long while before realizing this was the kind of front door no one ever used. So I went around back to the kitchen and knocked, nervous that Taddy Keegan was going to wonder what I was doing there. I saw the window above the driveway where Big Mori said Taddy's sister, Fiona, had jumped out one night trying to kill herself. But "no one can kill herself from a second-story window," Big Mori said. "It's just not high enough, even if you land on concrete."

Mrs. Keegan didn't ask who I was. She just stood for a moment beyond the darkened screen door in her white apron, and then her wide body faded away into the back of the kitchen. A few seconds later, Taddy appeared on the other side of the screen and waved me inside without really looking at me. I followed him through the dining room and across an empty living room into a small den, where two of his brothers and his dad were watching television. The brothers sat on the couch and Mr. Keegan sat in an armchair smoking a cigar, his eyes watery red, his thick black eyebrows flicking up and down as if he was trying to keep the smoke away from his eyeballs.

Taddy leaned on the couch arm next to Mr. Keegan, and the only place for me was behind the couch. So I stood there and watched TV with them. It was the show about Beaver that I didn't really like, because Beaver always got in trouble and then somehow got out of it in a way that didn't seem real.

Eddie Haskell knocked on the door—"Hi, Mrs. Cleaver. Where's the Beav?" "Upstairs," she said. So Eddie climbed the stairs and went into the boys' room, where Wally was sitting on top of Beaver on the bed, with Beaver's arms pinned under his knees. Wally was lightly slapping Beaver's face back and forth in a relaxed way, as if he had been doing it a long while and the Beaver was used to it. "Gee, Wally, whatcha doin'?" Eddie Haskell asked. "Ah, nuthin'," Wally said and shrugged. "Just giving Beav the business."

The voices inside the TV laughed. And then the Keegans laughed. And I faked a laugh, too.

When the ad came on, Taddy said, "C'mon. Let's go."

We left the den without anyone saying anything. As we walked away, we still heard the TV—something about a cereal you can buy that has a magic spoon inside. And I thought how different the Keegan house was from my house—how my father would never sit in the curtained dark on a Sunday afternoon and laugh at the Beaver show. Because he was too serious and unhappy in a way everyone could tell, just by looking at him.

When we reached the kitchen, Mr. Keegan started yelling at us from the den in an accented voice, with thick words I couldn't quite understand.

"Ah, he's doin' his Irish on us," Taddy said.

Taddy cut back into the living room. I followed and watched him talk loudly to his father in the same fake accent, Mr. Keegan "smiling devilishly," as my mother would say, with his curly black mustache and eyes lit up bright.

"Ah, me matey," Taddy said. "The thing is, we have to go."

"Ah, do ya have to now, lad? It makes me sad, you know. Your pa . . ."

"Ah, yes. And I love ya, Pa. But that's the way it is. And you can't change the way it is. Ma always tells ya that."

"Ah, so she does . . . It's a sad world then for a man like me."

"'Tis, Pa. But you're a big Killarney man."

"So I am . . . Give us a hug, then, laddie."

They hugged with only their shoulders touching, and patted backs, and touched chins with hands, like the whole scene had been performed before. Then it was over, and Mr. Keegan returned to the den and Taddy turned to me.

"C'mon," he said in a normal voice. "I want to show you something."

As we headed toward the back door, I wondered where the other Keegan children were—my mother made us say "children, because kids are baby goats." There were nine Keegan children. "Ten," my mother said, "if you count Mr. Keegan."

We crossed Mohawk Street and cut through a neighbor's side

yard until we came to the woods. Then we took the path leading to the top of Kaufman's Hill. We passed the toby tree, which no longer had any tobies, and stopped next to the hollow of another tree. Taddy reached inside and pulled out a crumpled pack of cigarettes that said "Benson and Hedges." He tapped out a long, slightly bent, white cigarette, and matches, and then lit the cigarette just like you see on TV, cupping his hands and puffing the smoke.

"Do you want one?" he asked, his lips tight and his eyes aiming up into the trees.

I watched as the light rain dripped off his nose and chin. Amazingly, his cigarette burned on.

"Where'd you get them?"

"From my mother. I take one every day from her packs lying around the kitchen. That way she never misses them. And I keep them inside this tree so they won't get wet. You can come here and smoke them any time you want. Just don't smoke them all."

"Is this what you wanted to show me?"

"No," he said, the smoke puffing out as he spoke.

I followed him farther down the path, the little clouds of smoke rising above the back of his head as he moved along, mixing in with the smell of the rain, like when my father smoked under the back porch when it was raining . . . after dinner, as he listened to the ballgame on his transistor radio, the smoke and rain mixing together and rising up like something holy, right through the falling sheets of darkness and passing into my open bedroom window, moving across my body as I lay on the bed without covers, and then across the hot bedroom and out the window on the other side, making everything cooler for a moment so you could let go and not have to worry about anything.

Near the edge of Kaufman's Hill, Taddy reached under some bushes and pulled out two wet truck-tire inner tubes. I could smell the black rubber before touching them.

"I told you I would get these from the gas station," he said. "We can blow them up and ride the creek. Have you seen the creek lately?"

"No," I said.

He slung one of the huge tubes over his shoulder, and I let him sling the other over mine. Then I followed him down the side of Kaufman's Hill toward Washington Road. As we approached the Big Intersection, the rain began falling harder, but Taddy and I didn't care.

The man at the Esso station let us blow up the inner tubes, just like Taddy said. I watched as he held the hose onto the tube nozzle, his eyes facing the asphalt where the rain puddles danced with the rainbow oil as the quick drops hit.

I thought about the long sewer tunnel right underneath our feet, and how I had gone all the way through it with Taddy back in October. And soon after that, the rainy day in November when I walked all the way home from St. Thomas More School for the first time, finally reaching the Big Intersection and cutting behind the Esso station . . . *because the principal's voice on the intercom said school was ending early and the buses weren't coming; and our parents weren't coming either because you can't call them all during a national emergency, so we'd have to walk home, making us think we were under attack from the sky, so we looked upward as we made our way across the parking lot in the rain and climbed the hill toward the aluminum building that was temporarily St. Thomas More Church, Sister Joseph standing in front and crying like she was afraid of going inside. "What's the matter, Sister?" I asked. But she wouldn't say, and then, a few seconds later, she felt too sad to care and told me anyway about the president being wounded in Texas and nobody knowing what to do.*

"I'm so sorry," she said over and over, making me feel sorry, too, but I didn't say because I was afraid of her crying; her hand reaching out like she was going to touch, and then drawing back, her body finally turning and disappearing into the aluminum church, maybe to pray to

the patron saint of presidents . . . and I joined back in with the stream of kids walking along Fort Couch Road, and then onto Washington Road, toward the long downhill leading to the Big Intersection that the President had driven through a year before, and my neighborhood that seemed farther away than I remembered . . . Washington Road isn't a walking road, my mother says, because there aren't any decent sidewalks and the four lanes of traffic don't care about who you are . . . with the rain falling steady and nobody caring about that either, walking in single-file without hardly talking, the sadness mixing inside the rain itself that seemed more like mist, hardly touching our hands, and the people going uphill in their cars staring ahead with faces you've never seen before, passing the strange line of school kids walking downhill, pretending not to notice them . . .

The blown-up tubes were bigger than we were. So we rolled them down Gilkeson Hill, past the Kaufman's Department Store site. At the steep part, Taddy let go of his tube on purpose. So I did, too, and we watched them crash through the trees above the creek.

"C'mon," Taddy said, running. "We have to get them before the creek takes them away."

Both inner tubes had stopped on the concrete above the big sewer tunnel. We dragged them behind us across the soggy grass above the creek, past the sewer entrance that led under the Big Intersection, until we found a spot Taddy Keegan liked.

The creek water was rushing huge, beyond the banks and into the trees. Up ahead, the tunnel under the Iroquois dead end was full almost to the top. And I couldn't see how we could possibly fit through. But Taddy was already preparing to get on top of his inner tube.

"This is where we'll start," he said.

"Have you done this before?" I asked.

"You just throw down the inner tube and hop on with your stomach at the same time. The current will take you. Once you get through the short tunnel, it's all open rapids on the other side, and we can ride them for a mile. I've checked it out. As long as you hold onto your inner tube, you'll be fine. That's why I got the truck-size ones. Nothing will touch us."

I could imagine myself riding the inner tube. I just didn't want to try and fit through the tunnel.

"Why don't we start on the other side?" I yelled.

But Taddy Keegan was already gone, his body rising up and down in the wild rushing, heading for the tunnel where the creek water was backwashing. At the last second, he ducked his head and the tube somehow dropped down, too, and he disappeared into the tunnel. And then it was strangely quiet, even with the sound of the rain and racing brown water.

I knew I shouldn't do it. But I kept thinking about how Taddy got a truck inner tube just for me, and kept it hidden for days until the rains came. And that's why he looked like he was expecting me when I showed up at his kitchen door. And how he had led me through the long sewer tunnel to the other side, and nothing bad happened. So why not ride an inner tube so large nothing can touch you?

The late afternoon seemed to turn darker and colder. Or maybe it was just the creek. Beyond the smell of the rain and the brown water, I smelled something else . . . making me tilt my head back so the drops hit my face.

I looked in the direction home, where I knew I wouldn't go, then threw my inner tube down, hoping it might float away like an accident. But I jumped on before it got too far, and landed with only my arms around the tube, the rest of my body in the cold creek water. I tried climbing onto my belly, like Taddy Keegan said, and that's when the tube started spinning. When I got close to the tunnel, the tube bobbed back and forth between the tunnel entrance and the backwash, like a pinball no one can control.

After a few seconds, I was sucked in like there was a cable pulling from underneath, and nothing could be done except keep my head down. There was no room for that, though, and the top of my head banged against the corrugated metal roof again and again, even with my cheek suctioned tight against the cool black rubber and my body wrapped around. So I closed my eyes and tried to imagine the creek spreading out in front of me like a bright field of low rippling water in the white sun, the water so wide that even Taddy Keegan appeared small, standing in dry clothes even though the ripples flowed silvery around his feet and pants legs, the water somehow never touching him.

The drop-down was like flying for a moment, taking your stomach away just beyond the tunnel's mouth, and then spinning around without moving downstream, until the invisible stick stopped the inner tube, but not me, during a single second when I forgot to hold on, and into the brown-smelling . . . *dragged like a doll against a tree limb that lay across the creek like a gate, that Taddy Keegan had already passed through, with the rushing smell of water in my nose and mouth, trying to drag me under, because that's where the current was heading; thinking maybe I should go there too, because there had to be a passage underneath, but still holding onto the log with both hands behind my head, as my mouth drifted under so I had to drink the brown water again and couldn't even say goodbye to mother and sisters and brothers, and father, too, because you can only drink creek water for so long unless the hand of God or Taddy Keegan comes crawling across a log and not even calling you by name but grabbing you by the hair, where the top of your head is bloody because of the corrugated tunnel roof, and lifting you up with the roughness of a man grabbing a dog by the neck, moving you sideways because you never thought of that or you could have saved yourself, instead of trying to hold on or dive underneath . . .*

All I had to do was move sideways to be free.

"You didn't hold on," Taddy said.

He didn't act as if he had saved me. He just seemed irritated because I had interrupted his creek ride.

"I did," I said, trying not to cry.

He walked away, hardly looking at me, toward his inner tube, which hung on a tree limb like a giant hat.

"Are we going home now?" I asked.

"You can. I'm going to finish the ride . . . and see if I can find your inner tube. It floated past me."

He pulled his inner tube down from the tree and walked back into the creek as if he were re-entering a swimming pool. As he disappeared around the bend, leaning up against a curl of brown water, he shouted something in Irish I couldn't understand.

The rain came down harder as I made my way home, my stomach feeling sick from the creek water like I wanted to throw up. But I wouldn't let myself, because I was afraid of losing control. So I held the sick water inside and walked slowly, hoping the rain would wash away the blood from the top of my head so my mother wouldn't see it, and I could just tell her I slipped into the creek by accident and got wet.

When I got home, I didn't feel like going inside. So I went around back to look at my garden. All the plants were flat against the mud. I should have tied up the tomatoes and corn with sticks, I thought, like Billy Creely probably did.

I didn't care anymore if he had poisoned everything. Because then the garden would go away and I wouldn't have to worry about it any more. And my father's backyard could return to the way it was, as if nothing had ever happened. And as if nothing had happened inside the creek water, too.

I realized I was standing in the same pose as my father when he first saw his dug-up lawn, shaking his head as if the world were ending. I wanted to cry but was afraid of my body. And then I didn't care about that, either, thinking that's how you know you're already dead: You don't care about anything—not gardens or backyards or families. And so maybe I had only dreamt of Taddy Keegan pulling me out of the drowning water, because he had to be way down the creek by then, *with the smoke and the rain mixing together and He rising up like He was going to walk with me . . .*

If only the rain really could wash everything away, and I could lie down and the grass and weeds would grow over me. And when Kenny Franz visited on Friday, I wouldn't have to worry about being nice to him.

Because Sundays really are the saddest days. Which I kept forgetting until Sunday came again. And Sunday evenings the worst of all. Because Sundays were meant for family. But the need for family never seemed like enough, since there was always something that family couldn't touch, but which I touched when I drank the creek water and which still touched me through the darkening air . . .

. . . as Taddy Keegan flies down the wild brown creek in the falling twilight, with nothing touching him, while I stand wishing it would rain so hard I can't breathe.

Kaufman's Field

When Kaufman's department store was finally finished the next spring, most of the woods around it were gone, except for at the top of Kaufman's Hill. They planted some thin grass underneath a layer of straw in the remaining field, in-between the large white shale rocks and some skinny trees they had planted the year before, and then they forgot about it. And everyone else started forgetting about how it used to be.

After school was over in June, my mother signed me up for golf lessons at the country club. "You're eleven," she said. "And they're teaching junior golf for children your age."

I didn't mind until I realized how much better the other boys were. They had played with their fathers for years, and they all knew each other and laughed in the same way after hitting their balls farther than I could imagine.

I kept playing with them on Monday mornings because I didn't want to hurt my mother's feelings. But I played secret golf by myself at Kaufman's Field in the evenings before dinner, hitting the ball out of the loose straw and aiming at the artificial-looking white rocks as imaginary holes. I didn't have to worry about anyone watching or bothering me, so I hit the ball better than on the real course at the country club.

One evening, though, I heard a *click* just before I hit my ball, and turned to see Billy Creely finishing his swing, aiming at the same white rock I was. He shot the ball well, even though the Creelys didn't play golf. And I remembered him bragging one time about how he could "play any sport great, without even practicing."

Billy kept on hitting without looking at me, and then walking serious, as if he was playing a real golf course. I wanted to leave, because I couldn't play Kaufman's Field golf with him there. But I didn't want Billy to think he could make me leave. So I hit my ball anyway, not very well, and tried to ignore him, hoping he wasn't watching me.

But he yelled out, "Hey, do you want to play a match? We could count our hits. I bet I can beat you."

I knew he probably could, so I left and started walking down the path toward the little kids' park that had recently been installed above the basketball court.

"I've got to go," I said, without looking back. "I'll play you another time."

But I knew I never would. And I knew I'd never take my golf clubs back to Kaufman's Field. Because Billy Creely had ruined that for good.

By mid-July, everyone was using Kaufman's Field. The Creelys had figured a way to play softball there using some of the rocks for bases and creating special rules for the little trees planted in the outfield. They organized the teams and we played in the late afternoons.

Taddy Keegan played, too, but he never paid much attention to the Creely rules. Whenever he ignored them, the Creelys laughed. But it was a different kind of laugh than when others laughed at Taddy Keegan. The Creelys laughed because they wanted to pretend they weren't bothered by the "crazy Irish kid," which is how Frank referred to Taddy Keegan when Taddy Keegan wasn't around.

One hot afternoon, Frank Creely batted a high fly ball, and Taddy Keegan started running around in little circles, screaming, in a TV cartoon voice, "I got it! I got it!"

At the last second, though, Taddy dropped his mitt and let the softball hit him, smack-loud on top of his head. The ball bounced about ten feet back into the air, and Taddy fell flat on his back in an exaggerated way and pretended to be dead.

Frank Creely froze for a few moments between first and second base, and then continued to run.

"That was the loudest smack ever!" I yelled from my position at second base.

A moment later, Taddy jumped back up as if he'd never felt anything.

"That's right, my boy!" he said in a scientific voice. "Now you know what the perfect smack sounds like."

The Creelys weren't happy because they thought Taddy Keegan wasn't taking their game seriously. So Frank ended the game early, due to "injury," he said. But Taddy Keegan was dancing around like a boxer.

After everyone left, Taddy climbed over the concrete wall into the cool dark of the Kaufman's underground garage, and I followed as he moved between the parked cars like he was looking for something and forgot what it was. *Maybe he really did hurt his head*, I thought.

But he was actually looking for cars with open windows and cigarettes left on the dashboard. Then he'd reach in to grab the half-empty packs, fast, like an animal.

After a couple minutes, he said, "OK, that's enough. Let's go."

We walked calmly toward the circular car ramps, jumped over the wall, and crossed the field toward Kaufman's Hill. We held onto the crown vetch like riding reins and pulled ourselves up the hill to

Taddy's rock.

After putting all the cigarettes into one pack, he lit one to smoke, a menthol. I asked if he liked menthols, and told him how my dad smoked Kools half the time, and L&Ms the other half—alternating, keeping the two packs in separate pockets and leaving the butt of the last one he had smoked on the lip of the ashtray in order to remember which brand was next. But Taddy Keegan didn't seem interested. He was concentrating on his smoking like it was hard work. Occasionally, he rubbed his head, as if remembering all over again that the fly ball had hit him there.

When he looked at me, it seemed by accident. Because his eyes always stared beyond, past everything. So I tried watching him sideways without him seeing, as the department store lights gradually came on and the sky faded into gray.

ᚦᚦᚦ

The next time we played softball, Taddy Keegan showed up with a small white rat on his head. It had squinty red eyes and looked dangerous. Still, Little Kenny Franz wanted to hold it.

"You can touch him, but that's it," Taddy said, bending over with the rat somehow still clinging against gravity onto his hair.

When Taddy played outfield, the rat stayed on top of his head, moving in little jerky circles as if it was afraid of falling, especially when Taddy ran to catch a fly ball. Meanwhile, the Creelys pretended the rat wasn't there, because they hoped Taddy would play worse with a rat on his head.

When it was Taddy's turn to bat, he finally put the rat down on the large white rock to the left of home plate that the Creelys designated the "on-deck" rock, where the next batter always had to stand. Taddy's rat moved a few inches in either direction but never left the rock. Little Kenny stared, still wanting to play with it.

"What's his name?" Kenny asked.

"I don't call him anything. He's not a pet," Taddy said, trying to focus on the spinning pitches coming from Frank Creely.

"He has to have a name," Kenny said.

"You can call him whatever you want, then," Taddy said, getting irritated.

Frank Creely, too, was losing his patience. "Play the damn game, will you?!" he yelled from the pretend pitcher's mound, which was nothing more than a circle of dirt and leaves.

Frank pitched again, and Taddy hit a line drive over Frank's head.

Little Kenny saw his chance: "C'mon, Mr. Rat. Don't you want to be held?" When he reached for the rat, it nipped at his fingers. I couldn't understand why Kenny would want to touch a rat anyway.

"Hey! Get off the on-deck rock unless you're up next!" Frank yelled to Kenny.

But it was little Kenny's turn to bat, and he slowly backed away from the rat to stand at home plate. Billy Creely, who usually played on Frank's team, took his place atop the on-deck rock. And I was up after him.

Frank was mad at Billy about something and traded him to our team as punishment, in exchange for Georgie-Porgie. It was a lousy trade, because Georgie-Porgie never hit anything out of the infield and was slow running the bases.

At first, Billy ignored the rat sharing the rock with him. But then he started giving it little kicks every time he thought Taddy, on second base, wasn't watching. Little Kenny was so worried about Billy hurting the rat that he couldn't concentrate on Frank's pitches.

And it seemed strange that Billy Creely, who was so great at everything, would be bothered by a small rat. And maybe that's why he didn't see little Kenny swing hard at the next pitch, nicking the ball foul toward third base but also letting go of the bat, which flew full force into Billy Creely's face, the smacking sound of the hard wood into his eye socket so sickening that my stomach caved in.

Time seemed to stop for a moment on Kaufman's Field. And when it started again, we couldn't recognize Billy Creely's face—his thick eyebrows and short forehead and dark hair all lost in the bloody mess spreading from his right eye. And Billy still standing while he screamed, his body dancing on the rock and his hands pressing against his eye with the blood running out between his fingers. And little Kenny still at home plate with his hand in front of his toothy mouth, saying over and over, "Oh my god, the bat just slipped, the bat just slipped . . ."

Frank Creely ran to home plate and punched little Kenny several times in the face and shoulders. And Kenny didn't even try to protect himself. Then Frank went to his brother, whose body had fallen on top of the rock and was jerking around beside the rat. His screams were louder and higher-pitched, his eye invisible through the purplish-red blood.

I heard someone say we should go into Kaufman's and call an ambulance, but no one moved. Next to Billy, Taddy's rat clung to the edge of the rock until Frank kicked it toward third base.

"I'm going to take him home, you sons of bitches!" Frank yelled, as if we were all at fault.

Then he and his youngest brother, Brian, picked up Billy and carried him under their arms like a rolled carpet, Billy still screaming and trying to cover his face, the sound of his screaming slowly diminishing as they moved down the little hill toward the Iroquois dead end.

I felt bad in a way you never forget, and sort of sick, too, because no one deserved to get hit in the face by a baseball bat, not even Billy Creely.

"Well, the game's over for today," Big Mori announced. "And there will be no more standing on the rock when someone's at bat."

I went to see little Kenny, who was sitting at home plate crying quietly, whether from the beating by Frank or from his guilt over throwing the bat—I couldn't tell. There was blood under his nose, but he didn't seem to care. I picked him up by the arm and told him I would walk him home, and he didn't seem to care about that either.

"When Mr. Creely calls," he mumbled, not looking at me, "my father is going to kill me."

"It was an accident, Kenny."

"That won't matter to my father," he said, his eyes in a trance. "He'll kill me just because Mr. Creely called him. He won't care about anything else."

I left Kenny in front of his house up on Gilkeson Road just as it was getting dark. But instead of going home, I found myself heading back to Kaufman's Field. In the dimming light, I could still see Billy's blood, black-looking on the gray-white rock.

I looked up toward Kaufman's Hill, and could make out the dark figure of Taddy Keegan sitting on his rock and the vague glow of his cigarette. I climbed up through the crown vetch darkness, and as soon as I reached the top, he offered me a cigarette. This time I said OK, and puffed lightly, because I had never smoked before and didn't want to cough.

"Is your rat still down on the field?" I asked. "Do you want me to help you look for him?"

"You can go look if you want," he said, as if it didn't matter.

I imagined finding the rat on my own and taking it to little Kenny, since Taddy didn't want it anymore, and the rat making Kenny feel better. But I just sat on the rock and didn't move because everything felt so ruined.

A minute later, Taddy stood up and threw his cigarette butt down into the vetch.

"Remember I told you I could fly off this hill?" he yelled suddenly, in a raspy, strange-sounding voice. "By squinting my body real hard. Because no one knows the truth about flying."

His voice scared me, so I stopped thinking about Little Kenny at his house and Billy Creely's smashed eye.

Taddy moved his legs to the edge of the crumbly yellow rock like he was going to try flying. I stood, but decided not to stop him this time. I wasn't afraid anymore about him falling down the crown bitch hill, but I was afraid that he might actually fly into the twilight and make me the boy who saw another boy fly, changing my life forever because a miracle like that can be worse than real life.

Instead, Taddy Keegan pushed me hard to the ground and called me a "fritzy coward." Then he went down the fading path into the woods and I lost sight of him.

I couldn't understand why Taddy got mad when I was going to let him fly, and mad before when I didn't.

I sat on his rock until the darkness seemed to come in like curtains all around, and the department store lights twinkled below in a way that bothered me. But I tried not to focus on that, or on the dinner hour, when I was supposed to be home before my father finished his drinks while pacing and smoking his two brands of cigarettes.

Every now and then, I turned around to see if Taddy Keegan was coming back down the path out of the darkness to the edge of Kaufman's Hill. But he never did.

Kreutzer's Pond

A couple weeks later, when I went back to the underground Kaufman's garage with Taddy Keegan, a man's voice reached us unseen, echoing from every direction: "Hey, you boys! Stop right there!"

We couldn't tell how far away he was, but I knew there was time to escape over the concrete wall. So I started to run, and then stopped, because Taddy wasn't moving. He looked relaxed, like he was thinking himself into some other place and didn't even hear the garage man's voice.

"Let's go, Taddy! We gotta run!" I yelled, but he still didn't move.

I could see the short stubby garage man approaching in a fast walk and wondered if I should take off by myself. But when the man was close enough for me to read "Beafhart Security" on his cap, I knew it was too late. So I pretended I didn't care, just like Taddy Keegan, who wasn't even looking at the Beafhart man.

He had a face that hadn't been shaved in a while and long gray hair that curled from under his cap. *Maybe he's been walking around this garage a long time*, I thought. *Or maybe he lives here.*

The man stood close in front of us, while Taddy smiled like something funny was going on.

"I watched you boys take cigarettes out of those cars," the Beaf-hart man said. "You're going to have to come with me now. We can go to the office and I'll call your parents, or I can call the police. Which do you want?"

Taddy still didn't say anything, so I kept quiet, too. But I tried looking at the man without him knowing. In my side-vision, I could also see the bright outside calling me from beyond the wall. Taddy continued to smile close-lipped, as if the security man's words didn't mean anything.

Long seconds passed, and the man's face turned impatient. He cast his eyes around as if checking to see if anyone was watching. But there was only a silver car driving up the ramp to the second level.

When Taddy finally spoke, he stared at the man for the first time.

"We're gonna go now, mister," he said in a cowboy voice, his mouth still smiling. "Thanks for that warning. It was mighty kind of you."

"I didn't give you a warning," the man shot back. "I said you have to come with me. Didn't you hear me?"

Taddy turned to go, and the Beafhart man grabbed his shoulder.

"Mister, if you don't let go, I'll scream so loud your whole family will hear me," Taddy said in a calm cowboy way. "You don't want that, now do ya, mister?"

The Beafhart man said nothing. His eyes seemed to lose all expression. Taddy held the pack of cigarettes right in front of the man's nose.

"And I got these from me mammy," Taddy said in a different TV voice. "I takes them from me mammy so the lass won't toke so much. Do ya see, laddy?"

The man let go, looking confused. And Taddy Keegan turned to walk toward the wall like he forgot I was there too. I followed, and we swung ourselves over the ledge into the shocking afternoon light.

"Look back at him," Taddy said in his normal voice. "I bet he's still standing in the same place. Right?"

And the Beafhart man was, as if he couldn't figure what to do next. When I looked back a second time, I couldn't see him anymore. Maybe he was hidden inside the garage shadow.

After that, I didn't see Taddy until school started in September, and he seemed different than in the summer. He didn't pay much attention to me, and I wasn't sure if it was because I had been afraid of the Beafhart man or because of something else. All I knew was that when I saw him on the St. Thomas More playground, I felt more sad than ever about summer being over.

After a while, I realized it wasn't just me. Taddy Keegan wasn't paying attention to anyone. Maybe it was because of the bald spot on the top of his head that everyone said was caused by the rat he used to keep there. Some started calling him "the monk." But a monk's patch is smooth and normal-looking, whereas Taddy's was flaky-white with red bumps.

Big Mori called him "Disease Head," but not to Taddy's face. And through Taddy's distant eyes, I could see he didn't care what anyone thought about his bald spot. I just kept hoping his hair would grow back and Taddy would return to the way he was before. Just like I hoped Sister Helen would stop calling me "Skinny" in front of our sixth grade class. But she never would. Even after I stopped raising my hand to answer, she'd call on me anyway: "So, Skinny, what do you think?" she'd say.

And I guess it was all right for a nun to say that because I really was skinny. And that's why I'd stuff handkerchiefs into my back pockets in the morning to make it look like there was something back there. But when my Uncle Al visited, who was a Jesuit priest in

Tokyo, he'd still throw me over the back of the couch and, with his red hands and long fingers, pretend to spank me, saying, "Pants with nothing in them! Pants with nothing in them!"

Later in the evening, my mother would tell me not to worry about being thin, because I'd grow up tall, which would be a fine thing. But I couldn't believe in that.

One day at recess, Taddy asked me to slap his bald spot to see if it would make that perfect smacking sound. And I didn't want to, because I didn't want to feel his hairless patch and the little red bumps with my bare hand. But then I thought about how he could have chosen someone else to smack the top of his head, so maybe I was special after all. And that's why I decided to smack him whenever he asked me to, right in front of the other boys. It didn't feel like the right thing to do, and it made me feel sick through my hand from his prickly-bare skin. And it didn't even make that perfect smacking sound. But he kept having me do it anyway, all because a white rat had made his scalp sick from living on his head too long.

The other kids were amazed I could hit Taddy Keegan and get away with it. And I just thought it was a strange way for me and Taddy to play.

〢〣〤〢〣〤

Near the middle of October, I saw him down by the creek in the late afternoon with a slingshot in his hand. He was whittling the handle with a penknife. Then he stopped to test it, shooting a creek-pebble up into the colored leaves.

I walked close enough that he had to see me, but I focused straight ahead so he would think I didn't see him. I pretended to pick something up off the grass, to slow myself down. But he still didn't call out to me. Eventually, I had to walk past him.

When I turned around, he was standing on a rock with his back to me. A few seconds later, I turned a second time and he was gone.

At home, I took my father's rusty saw off the shelf in the garage and went up to my third-floor bedroom, which used to be my older brother's room, and took his Boy Scout knife out of the desk drawer. Then I got a few thick rubber bands from my mother's junk drawer in the kitchen.

My father wasn't home from work yet, and my mother was down in the laundry room, so I headed out through the kitchen unseen and went into the backyard of the house next-door, where the Kreutzers used to live. They were an unfriendly family, like the Hartmans across the street. My father said it was because they were both Protestant. But that didn't stop my brother from watching Diane Kreutzer through the living room window every time she got in and out of her blue Pontiac.

The Kreutzers were going to build a more modern house where their fish pond was. My parents said it didn't make sense. But I heard Mr. Kreutzer on the phone one time, his voice coming into our den from his kitchen window, talking about how his old house was too dark and depressing, like most houses in Pittsburgh. And he wanted more light.

I walked between their thick trees to the empty fish pond and wondered what Mr. Kreutzer had done with his old carp fish. Maybe he had taken them to the Monongahela River, where they could live with the other carp fish downtown.

From under the tree shadows in the early twilight, I tried to imagine them swimming in the pond again, peaceful and pale orange, flicking fast beneath the autumn leaves scattered across the dark surface.

Sometimes I would sneak over to watch them, sitting on the circular stone wall and staring into the foggy water. Some people thought Mr. Kreutzer's fish were ugly and called them "garfish." But I didn't think so.

One time he came out of his house and I thought he was going to yell at me. But he just stared through his thick glasses with the black frames and talked about how tiny goldfish can turn into big carp. "Fish always grow to the size of their container," he said.

The stone floor of the pond was dry now, except for some moisture near the edges of a few dark leaves. I could smell dampness in the air, inside the shadows of the overhanging trees.

When I was certain no one could see me from the street, I began sawing at the base of one of the tree branches that extended into a Y shape. After a few seconds, I stopped because the noise was louder than I expected.

I had never used a saw before, and never seen my father or brothers use one. So I worried about whether I was doing it right, and about it being too dark in the Kreutzer's backyard for me to see OK. But I started up again, and didn't stop until the branch broke free.

On the ground, I sawed off the two smaller branches and the slingshot fell away, as if it had always been there hidden inside the branch and just needed to be set free.

The whittling of the handle was easier because my brother's knife was still sharp. The bark shot off in shavings that disappeared into the Kreutzer's pond, making no sound. With my feet dangling over the edge, I thought I could still smell the carp somehow.

I heard Mr. Frankel's wiener dog barking out on the sidewalk and was afraid it might come around to find me. So I froze still for a while, until I was sure Mr. Frankel and his dog had walked past.

When the handle felt smooth, I stopped, wondering how to carve the notches at the top of the two posts where the rubber bands would go. And I had no idea how to tie the rubber bands because I was terrible at making knots. Maybe I should have stayed in Cub Scouts after all, I thought, like my brother. But after accidentally spitting water on Mrs. Schetzke, the den mother, they made me leave.

My left hand shook as I tried sawing the notch, and the sweat began to drip down the underside of my arms. I paused, and could smell the mossy dampness coming from the empty dark pond hole. For a moment, I thought I could even see the carp fish again, glowing orange inside a dimming green light.

I tried kneeling on the slingshot handle and that seemed to work better, even though the rock ledge was uneven. I finished one notch and started the other. Then I heard my father's black Oldsmobile pull into our driveway, and realized I had lost track of time underneath the Kreutzer trees. Soon they'll be wondering about me, I thought.

I remained still, listening for my father to close the heavy car door . . . and waited the long seconds for his slow walk up the stairs, and the opening and closing of the front door, as if for the final time.

When the quiet returned, I didn't quite feel like myself. But I continued carving, with the fish smelling all around in the cooling dark even though there weren't any fish to smell, until the notch was finished.

I decided to try and connect the rubber bands later, up in my room. So I jumped into the empty pond and felt around in the dark for some small stones, and packed them inside my right pants pocket. Then I folded up the penknife and stuffed it inside my left pocket.

After my parents and sister are in bed, I can fire into the darkness from my bedroom window, I thought. I just have to ease the copper window screen up without letting it snap. And I don't have to worry about where the stones land, because the old poplar trees in our backyard will catch them, so nothing would get hurt, except maybe some sleeping birds you can't see so you can't worry about. And the stones that made it through would land in a place no one can hear. If I can just figure how to tie the notches, even if it doesn't look as good as Taddy Keegan's . . .

The handle felt solid to my touch. Maybe I had picked a good branch after all. Some of the bark was still on the bottom, but that was OK because it made the slingshot easier to grip.

I brushed the tree shavings off my legs so my mother wouldn't see and slid the slingshot inside the back of my shirt, then tucked my shirt in. I hoped my mother and father were still having drinks in the living room so I could make it upstairs without them saying anything.

I wouldn't tell Taddy Keegan about my slingshot, because he might think I was copying him, which is something Billy Creely would do. But that meant me and Taddy would never shoot them together into the colored creek leaves.

When I reached our driveway, I remembered the saw. It was too late to put it back in the garage without my parents knowing, so I decided to leave it at the bottom of Kreutzers' pond, where no one would notice it against the rotting black leaves.

I can come back tomorrow, I thought, *and put it back in its spot in the garage. So I don't have to worry about the saw anymore.*

I didn't expect Little Kenny to be tagging along when I took my slingshot to the top of Kaufman's Hill, especially since he had stopped coming by on Friday nights. But he had seen me cutting through the houses on Mohawk Drive and followed behind.

"Did you make it yourself?" he asked, as we headed down the path through the woods. "What are you going to do with it?"

I didn't want him to see what I was doing, because I wasn't sure what I was going to do.

It was already after six o'clock and starting to get dark. I wished Little Kenny was home having his dinner like he was supposed to. Maybe something happened with his parents again, like the time his father, who had arms too big for the rest of his body, yelled over and over again at his mother until she just sat down in the middle of the kitchen floor and Kenny was told to leave the house. But this time, I didn't want to hear, because six to seven was my time—when I could go out and do whatever I wanted and not run into anyone, because they were all having their dinner while my family didn't eat until seven, after my father got home and had his highballs.

As we came out of the trees at the top of Kaufman's Hill, the air lightened a little. I sat down on Taddy Keegan's rock and didn't say anything, hoping Kenny would go away if I ignored him. But he sat next to me. I considered saying something to make him leave, but I knew I would feel bad afterwards.

The birds batted in and out of the trees behind us, swooping into the heavy dusk air hanging off the hill and then noisily returning. And then again . . . little black marks across a fading gray paper, getting too dark to see.

I wanted to yell at them. But that was something Dickie Labeau would do. I might have yelled anyway, except that Little Kenny was there.

I knew the birds were just trying to find a place to sleep. But they didn't have to make such a big deal about it. And why weren't they migrating south like the rest of the birds, instead of jabbering about nothing inside a faded-out sky? It was already November.

I looked at Kenny, who was fussing with the glasses on his nose. He didn't seem to care about the birds. And then a sense of emptiness dropped over me . . . I didn't know why I was there.

"Are you going to shoot one of the birds?" Kenny asked through a toothy smile I could almost see.

I hadn't thought about shooting the birds. I had just taken my slingshot with me to practice at night.

When I didn't answer, Kenny lowered his head as if he was going to fall asleep. I could see his hunched shape against the dark trees. The birds, too, had settled down.

"I guess I'll go home," he said suddenly, lifting his head back up.

"Wait until I'm down the hill before you shoot at anything."

He seemed relieved to go. And I felt relieved, too, and listened as he shifted his way down Kaufman's Hill more quickly than expected, through the nearly invisible crown vetch, falling a few steps, then moving slowly again, never voicing a sound. I thought of shooting a stone near him just for fun, to see if he would notice. But I didn't.

When I couldn't hear him anymore, I decided to shoot, just once, at the birds that had started up again. Not really aiming at anything, I pinched two stones between the rubber bands and shot them into the darkening air.

I waited to hear the stones land on Kaufman's parking lot, hoping they wouldn't hit the hood of a car. But I didn't hear anything.

Then, in the thick silence, there was a chirping sound about ten feet below. And it made me feel sick inside. Not in the way you want to throw up, but in a way where your whole body wants to desert you.

I knew I would never be able to find the bird inside the dark hill, even if I wasn't too afraid to touch it. And I wished I could go back to where I was before I fired my slingshot. But you can never do that.

The Kaufman's parking lot lights came on all at once, like someone knew what I had done. And it scared me. I stared at them for a while and tried to forget about the bird, but found myself counting off the beats until the next chirp, which came about every eight seconds from the hollow darkness below. *Some animal is going to hear you*, I wanted to say. *And then you will be eaten.*

Kaufman's Hill didn't feel the same, and neither did Taddy Keegan's rock.

I promised never to use my slingshot again, but that didn't help. So I considered throwing it down into the crown bitch, where the bird chirped higher pitched, and more weakly, like death was slowly winning out.

Maybe I should toss some rocks to make it shut up, I thought.

But I didn't do that either, as I felt my heart press against me and the sweat starting, even though it was too cold to sweat.

If only little Kenny had stayed, I thought. *Then I wouldn't have fired my slingshot at something I couldn't even see . . .*

Before I could feel myself get up, I was already standing on the crumbly white rock that looked chalky yellow in the dim light, just as I had seen Taddy Keegan do at dusk when he threatened to fly by squinting his body real hard in the air.

But it was nighttime now, and I couldn't see where to fly inside the closing window of Kaufman's Hill. The crown vetch dropped away unreal, gray and blurry, as if getting ready to disappear for good into the damp-smelling air.

And that's when I jumped into the crown bitch hill, slanting away with no color, forgetting even to try the hard body-squinting that Taddy Keegan talked about, because maybe I really wanted to fall.

. . . and it was like dropping into water when you let your body go limp, then awake at the last second and arch your back because that's probably what Taddy Keegan meant. Because he was right, people don't try hard enough . . . and that's why Taddy Keegan wouldn't have fallen with shame into the crown vetch hill smelling of rotten honeysuckle all over with sprained wrist and nose-breathing stopped almost so you can't see, but not crying in the alone . . . And still lying in the closing darkness waiting for God knows who but not wanting even Him to come because that would be worse, until you can't keep count of the insects climbing over you but not moving to scratch because you are afraid and deserve them anyway for failing to believe . . . Thinking how Taddy Keegan would be flying, like the miracles of Jesus that were witnessed only by those who could handle it, Sister Helen said . . . and wondering if anyone happened to look up through the silver dusk from Kaufman's parking lot to see a boy diving from the top of a gray hill, and then holding his breath for the longest time, crumpled inside the

crown vetch world, unwilling to move with the evening's dampness all over and everything crawling around . . .

I wanted to stay in the crown vetch world forever, and daylight to never come. And I never wanted to see Taddy Keegan again, or the stupid slingshot I had left on the yellowing rock at the top of Kaufman's Hill. I didn't even want to see my family again, because what would I tell my mother about my scratches and nose-bleeding that she would notice in the dim living room light as I passed my way to the stairs?

The bird chirped once more, right near me, its sad sound almost at arm's length. I kept hoping it would stop, so we could be quiet together.

Still I didn't move . . . thinking about Sister Helen telling us the story of the prophet Elijah, who survived the desert because the ravens came and brought him drops of water in their beaks. One drop at a time, over and over, until he had the strength to make it home.

I didn't really believe Sister Helen, but I still wanted the ravens to come for me, and save me from the crown vetch vines growing on top and collapsing underneath.

After a while, I didn't hear the bird anymore and thought maybe everything was finally over. But then the weak sound started up again, almost near enough for me to touch.

Gilkeson Road

Katy Casady was the girl I saw for the first time, standing and swaying next to Taddy Keegan one day at the bus stop, near the end of our sixth grade year.

He didn't seem to notice she was there, and I wanted to be that natural with her. Katy Casady . . . with the pixie-cut shiny black hair and round, untouched face.

I knew where she lived—near the bottom of Sunnyhill. I had watched her go into her dark red-brick house, shaded by bushes and trees so you could hardly see the front door. And maybe that's why Mrs. Casady drove her blue station wagon all the way up the crumbly-asphalt driveway to the back door, as I saw one day when I was walking down Sunnyhill with my skateboard under my arm so it looked like I had purpose, even though I was afraid to ride down Sunnyhill because it was too steep.

As the door opened and Mrs. Casady's leg dropped out, I was already laying my skateboard on the thin shade-grass and walking toward the back of her car, where the brown grocery bags waited— more groceries than my mom would ever buy because there were more Casadys.

"Can I help you carry your bags?" I asked from behind Mrs. Casady, who was bending over.

She didn't seem surprised I was there. Maybe other kids had asked to carry her bags before, since she had seven daughters.

I told her my name, hoping she would think I was a nice boy. But Mrs. Casady didn't seem to care that much, and just nodded and dropped two of the Kroger bags into my thin arms. Then she grabbed two herself, and we headed toward the Casady back door.

I was nervous about tripping on the rocky asphalt, and kept looking around the grocery bags to see my feet. Meanwhile, Mrs. Casady moved farther ahead, and the screen door opened and closed before I got there. So I juggled the bags on one arm and reached for the handle and stepped in, the screen door slamming behind and throwing me into the kitchen, making me spill some of the Scott toilet paper rolls onto the floor. Mrs. Casady looked once and then resumed putting the groceries away.

I picked up the toilet paper and stood there in the strangeness—being inside the Casady house without Katy Casady knowing it. I had never even spoken to her.

Her house smelled different than other houses. Because every house smells its own way, and you can never imagine that smell ahead of time. People move away, and their new house smells the same. Like the Portneys, who moved to a bigger house up on the brick-street hill. But their new house smelled just like their old one. House smells don't come from the house, but from the people living inside, mixing it all up.

The phone rang, and Mrs. Casady walked into the hallway to answer, leaving me alone. I could still see part of her body and hear her talking, but couldn't figure what she was saying.

If it's a short call, I thought, *I'll wait. But if it's a long call, I don't know what I'll do.*

As the seconds stretched out, I fought off thinking that I had no reason for being there. The Casady groceries had been delivered and I was just standing inside a strange house where people I didn't know happened to live. But when my mother would see the Casadys at Mass, she would mention how cute the seven girls were, so Katy Casady had to be all right.

In the hallway, Mrs. Casady moved the heavy black receiver to her other ear. That's when I decided to leave. But as I touched the screen door, Mrs. Casady yelled, "Katy!"

I wondered how she knew Katy was the one I wanted, and not Darcy, who was one year younger.

Across the kitchen, a staircase led to the upstairs bedrooms. Her bare feet appeared there first, then her head dropped upside-down with her black hair hanging gravity-loose and swaying a bit. She looked at me, and then back across the kitchen, as if still wondering what her mother wanted.

Mrs. Casady continued to talk on the phone.

"I helped your mother bring the groceries in."

She stared, still upside-down, and didn't say anything.

"I gotta go now," I said hurriedly.

The screen door accidentally slammed behind me—Mrs. Casady probably didn't like that—and then I started to run. But I stopped when I realized Katy might be watching through the window. So I fast-walked, realizing how difficult it is to walk straight when you're actually thinking about it.

I kept my head down, not looking back until I reached the stop sign at Seminole Drive. Then I remembered my skateboard and had to go back to the Casadys' lawn to get it. As I returned, I never looked at her house, because I didn't want to know if she was watching. And it didn't matter, because Katy Casady had probably already forgotten me—a strange boy who carried her mother's groceries and had nothing to say.

During the next few weeks, I watched from my sister's bedroom window for Katy Casady to leave after her babysitting job across the street where the O'Carrols used to live. When I was six years-old, I used to go over there all the time and play with Mattie O'Carrol. Until one day Mrs. O'Carrol sat me down on the stoop and explained how I was too old to play with girls anymore. And so I was condemned into the Creely's world.

If I saw Katy Casady leave the house, I'd rush downstairs and pretend to do something out in the front yard just to see if she would speak to me. And one evening she did, her black straight hair shifting forward as she made her way down the steep front lawn. Her voice sounded familiar, as if I'd heard it for years.

"What are you doing?" she asked.

"I'm going down to the creek," I said.

I hadn't planned on going anywhere, but the creek was the only thing I could think of.

"Do you want to go?"

"I haven't had my dinner yet," she said, looking up the street toward her house.

"Neither have I. We eat late."

She didn't say anything. And I couldn't see her face because her dark bangs kept falling across it as she kicked at the sidewalk with her shoe.

"Well, I'm going then," I said, my voice cracking just a bit.

I was almost past the Kreutzers' new house, built on top of where their fishpond used to be, when I heard her voice again:

"Why would I want to go to the creek?" she half-yelled.

"Because I could show you something there," I answered, without fully turning around.

So Katy Casady decided to miss her dinner and walk with me down Iroquois Drive, which seemed a lot longer than usual. Every now and then, I'd glance across, but her hair remained slanted and I couldn't see her face. So I watched her feet instead—black and white saddle shoes moving beneath a brown skirt that I wanted to touch.

At the dead-end circle, we crossed the asphalt path leading to Kaufman's and headed down the embankment toward the creek. The over-green smell of May was everywhere inside the high grass and damp weeds along the bank. And it seemed to be getting darker sooner than normal. Maybe it was just the clouds.

I sensed Katy Casady really did expect me to show her something at the creek. Something amazing—but there was just the thick green weeds and brown water.

Above us, we heard sirens on Gilkeson Road.

"I wonder what's going on," she said.

"Maybe there's a fire somewhere," I said, not really interested in the sirens.

Katy Casady looked up as if she wanted to figure it out. And I was afraid she would leave and ruin everything.

"Let's go to the sewer tunnel," I said, trying to bring her back.

She followed me along the creek edge, past the basketball court that Kaufman's built because they felt bad about taking away our woods. I stepped onto the big creek rocks and she followed, and didn't seem afraid of slipping. Up on Gilkeson Road, the sirens continued to moan.

I wanted to take her hand as we reached the mouth of the tunnel, and pretend it was because I didn't want her to fall. But I didn't, and we made it to the concrete slab and held onto the metal bars at the opening.

The sirens continued to whine as I watched the water rush around my feet and smelled the damp sewer air drifting into our faces.

"That tunnel goes all the way through," I said loudly. "All the way under Kaufman's and Gilkeson Road, and past the Big Intersection. Then it comes out on the other side in some woods. Have you ever been over there?"

She shook her head. But I couldn't tell if she hadn't been there or wasn't interested.

"I went all the way through one time. It was completely dark and I didn't know when it was going to end. And there were animals you can't see."

"Did you go alone?"

She looked at me for the first time, her hand almost touching mine on the sewer grate.

"I was with Taddy Keegan."

She turned in the direction of her home as if she wanted to leave. And that's when the sirens all of a sudden stopped. But it took a while to notice. And then we heard the traffic again on the newly widened roadway above us.

She stepped back and stood on a large rock, and I followed and stood on a rock next to hers.

"You weren't afraid of getting sick in there?" she asked, squinting her eyes at me. "Because rats live in sewers. That's why I would never go in."

"I figured I only had to go halfway. Then it's the same distance either way, so you may as well go on."

"But how did you know when you were halfway?"

Everything seemed quiet then, with the sirens over and the creek hardly making any noise, and the dusk gathering under the trees. Even the sewer smell seemed fine.

"I better be going," she said. "My parents will be wondering . . . Did you know we're moving in two weeks?"

"Moving?"

"We're moving to Columbus, Ohio. My dad got transferred. My sisters are crying about it, but I don't care. I don't think Columbus will be that different."

"I'll come and see you," I blurted out. "As soon as I turn sixteen and get my license. I'll drive there to see you."

"You'll never remember me by then."

"I will. You don't know me. I promise."

She was really looking at me, her black eyes weakening the backs of my legs. No one looked like that before, turning the creek world still. Even the damp-smelling tunnel seemed to no longer exist.

Something bothered my ear and so I moved my hand to scratch. Then she touched my ear, resting her arm on my shoulder from across the water.

"You're bleeding," she said calmly. "I think it was a spider. I can still see some of its legs."

I looked at my finger and the blood was there. And I could feel the wet in my ear. But it didn't bother me, standing under the darkening trees with the overgrown branches crowding around, because at dusk all the spiders come out.

One minute we were standing there, and the next I wanted to touch her cheek. But I was worried because of my hand with the blood. So I leaned over, across the creek water, to kiss instead. She looked up and our lips touched unevenly, so I couldn't tell if she actually kissed back. Because who can tell that? But I felt her cheek for a moment.

Then we were both standing on our rocks again, and I could hear the creek water again, louder than before. And Billy Creely's voice yelling from across the embankment. I worried that he had seen us and would ruin everything in the Creely way. And there was no escape. Not from the middle of the creek with him on the only side we could jump to.

"Mrs. Franz is dead!" he yelled. "Do you believe that? In the garage. Hung herself in the garage. Little Kenny found her. And I was the first one there. I heard the sirens and ran all the way to Gilkeson. The cops are there now."

He didn't seem to notice Katy Casady, as if he were staring straight through her. And I didn't believe him. Except why would a

Creely make something up like that?

When I didn't answer back, he moved on, past the shadows of the trees until I couldn't see him anymore. But I could hear his feet for a while landing on the twigs along the creek bank.

I looked back for Katy, but she had left her rock and was standing at the creek edge with her hands under her arms. Suddenly I was afraid for everything—Little Kenny's mom, Billy Creely seeing us, and for Columbus. I was mad at myself for telling Katy Casady I would drive there. Because she didn't believe me.

It would be easy to do. Just take the turnpike and—

"I'm going home now," she said. "Do you think that kid was telling the truth?"

"I can walk with you," I said.

"You should go up to Gilkeson and see what happened."

Before I could say anything, she was heading up the embankment, putting her hands on the ground to make sure she wouldn't slip. And then the overhanging branches blocked my view, and I couldn't see Katy Casady anymore.

It was past dinnertime, but I wasn't going home and I wasn't going to Little Kenny's. Mr. Franz scared me, and I didn't want to see his garage.

I climbed up to Gilkeson Road and walked the other way, but kept looking back toward Little Kenny's house. There was a police car parked in front, just as Billy Creely had said. But after a while, I could hardly see the car or the Franz house in the falling darkness.

I walked more quickly toward the Big Intersection, thinking that a fast pace might keep me from seeing Mrs. Franz in my mind— a thin woman with short, uneven hair and glasses, who stayed in the kitchen the one time I was there.

I deserve to see her in the garage, I thought, *for all the times I treated Little Kenny lousy.* Especially when he used to come by on Friday evenings and I didn't feel like playing with him, with my mother always saying "how easy it is to be kind." And I never had a reason not to be. And that's why I should have been in the darkened garage that smells like garages always do—of gasoline and damp cement, and of something else . . .

. . . *The light switches on and suddenly she is there, suspended perfectly still . . . but after a while, she seems to sway just a bit, which you hardly notice until you move up close, because gravity in union with the movement of the earth can tilt a dead woman inside a dark garage . . . while Katy Casady reaches home and has her late dinner alone at the kitchen table, then up to her bedroom where her sisters wait, not telling them about the boy who kissed her and hardly remembering how they touched cheeks over the creek water, forgetting already that he promised to drive to Columbus . . . leaving high school one day in his mother's Buick Special with extra food taken from the cafeteria, and finding the turnpike after heading east, which is the wrong direction, but the only way he knows after watching his father . . . and asking some gas station man just to make sure because his mother always told him never to be afraid to speak up . . .*

And the new Casady house would look different, made of wood instead of brick, and sitting in a sunny flat space with a bare yard, like those you see in the new suburbs, but it would still smell the same as the old Casady house . . .

And there wouldn't be any creek nearby, or tunnel, because there aren't any hills, and no Billy Creely coming along with the news of Little Kenny's mother, whose body you can't see while the light is off . . .

I toot the horn, even though my mother doesn't like us doing that, and the front door opens. Katy Casady is coming outside . . .

The lights had come on across the Big Intersection without me noticing, the Esso station lit up the brightest, with the cars moving in and out as if they were in a hurry to keep going. Bowling City was lit up, too, but I never liked going there, because inside spaces feel sad under fluorescent lights. Fluorescence turns dark things brown, Mr.

Schiezer, our science teacher, told us. Fuscous, he called it. Brownish gray, like the color of soil inside caves.

Kaufman's, too, was lit up across the parking lot, because people want to shop on Thursday nights. And beyond, there were the dark spaces you can't see, where Kaufman's Hill stands.

I sat on the same curb I had sat on before, at the intersection of Washington and Gilkeson Roads. So close I could feel the car engines breathing warm against me as they stopped for the red light, making me tired and wanting to lie down. But someone would come along and say, "Hey! You can't do that here." Even though the passing drivers would hardly notice.

I was near the halfway point of the sewer tunnel below, and could see a manhole cover in the middle of the street leading down to where I once was, the black metal shining at me every time a headlight passed.

I could go out there right now, I thought, and dodge the cars and lift the grate, and climb down to where Taddy Keegan and I used to be—to where it doesn't matter anymore, because it's the same distance either way, going back or going on. And Katy Casady, whose cheek I wanted to touch with my hand, must have understood that.

The Back Porch

After Katy Casady moved away, the other Catholic school girls seemed to disappear as well, and by July we were hanging out with the public school girls for the first time, even though our parents told us not to in a way that was in-between words.

We'd meet after dinner, with no one in charge, under a spreading oak tree on the front lawn of a small corner house on Mohawk Drive. The house wasn't ours, but we knew the old lady who lived there would never say anything.

Each evening, it felt like we were meeting by accident—me and Georgie-Porgie and Taddy Keegan at the dead-end time of day in the middle of the Pittsburgh summer, sitting on the dew-grass under the oak tree, trying not to feel the wetness seeping through the bottoms of our pants.

We watched for the streetlights to come on to see who could spot them first, which is why we hardly noticed the group of girls heading our way from Marla Hawkins' house across the street until they stood right over us under the thick shadows of the tree.

We didn't say anything because we didn't know them very well— dark-haired Marla Hawkins; big-chested Carol Bradenton, whom

Big Mori called Care-hole; and a pretty girl named Nina. But we had heard about Marla Hawkins's older sister, Tina, who took boys up to her bedroom when her parents weren't home.

When Taddy Keegan finally stood up and spoke, it was as if he wasn't talking to us, but giving a speech somewhere, his voice serious, but in his fake-acting way.

"My older brother Paddy told me that if you take ten deep breaths, and hold the last one real long while someone squeezes you hard, you pass out for a while. And when you wake up, you don't know where you are."

I wasn't interested in passing out. But the girls wanted to try it without us even asking. So Marla Hawkins sat in front of me, and Nina in front of Georgie-Porgie, which didn't make any sense, and Carol Bradenton in front of Taddy. I could smell the back of Marla Hawkins' blue checkered shirt, she was so close and between my legs. But I was afraid to touch her, even though I knew I had to.

Some birds scattered out of the branches overhead like they had gotten scared. But I hadn't done anything wrong yet, except watch the back of Marla Hawkins's shoulders heave upward and downward as she took deep breaths in the near-darkness, her breathing growing louder until I forgot which number she was on.

I wanted to see what Taddy and Georgie were doing, but was afraid to take my eyes off Marla. So I turned for just a second and saw, through the gray air, Taddy Keegan squeezing Carol Bradenton. Still, I wasn't touching Marla, even though she had taken her last breath and was holding it, waiting for me, her hair smelling all around and her shoulders frozen in a hunched position.

I wished Taddy Keegan had explained things more, or that I had talked to his older brother, Paddy, when he was sitting in his taxicab in front of their house singing his Irish songs.

Marla's body felt thinner than I expected. And as I squeezed, her shoulders collapsed in a way that didn't seem natural. It was is if her inside shell couldn't protect the outer perfumed flesh, except for her breasts on the other side, which were lifted by my forearms so that I could feel the balance of them even though I wasn't supposed to, making me forget how long I had been squeezing her because Taddy Keegan never told us how long that was supposed to be.

When I finally let go, she was already falling back against me, heavier than I anticipated. *Maybe she's fooling around*, I thought.

I tried waking her by jiggling her shoulders. Then I shook her whole body with my legs. But still she fell back against me, her head lolling to the side and her hair spreading across the dark lawn. I remained on my elbows, feeling the wet grass and staring through the black leaves, hoping the long moment would end, unless I deserved it for doing something really wrong.

Taddy Keegan was laughing, and Carol Bradenton was giggling. But I didn't want to look over because I didn't want to miss Marla Hawkins, who was squeezing my hand, her warm body still on top of me. Then it seemed like she was actually pushing against me. So I let my arms buckle and lay back against the damp grass. She continued to squeeze my hand, and I wasn't sure if it was because she was angry or because she was trying to find her way back from not remembering where she was.

A long time seemed to pass with her on top of me, enough for the others to come and stand over us. Marla Hawkins wasn't making any noise, but I knew she was awake, and she wasn't getting up, either, even though she was back from where she didn't know she had been.

I finally squeezed her hand in return and closed my eyes so I didn't have to see Georgie-Porgie and Taddy. And we stayed like that for a while.

᚛ᛗᚨᛗᚨ᚜

Georgie-Porgie said we'd blown it—that we should have felt them up while they were passed out, that they wanted us to, that they expected us to . . .

He was pacing back and forth in front of the TV at Taddy Keegan's house, gesturing with his hands. And he kept saying "ipso facto," an expression he'd learned from his father.

"The girls asked us to squeeze them until they passed out, right? So, *ipso facto*, they wanted us to feel them up. And, *ipso facto*, they wanted to be unconscious when we did it so they wouldn't remember and couldn't be blamed for doing anything bad."

But we'd remember it, I wanted to say to Georgie-Porgie.

The next evening, we met in front of Taddy Keegan's house as the air was turning gray. After cutting through some side-yards, we came to the old lady's corner house, where the girls were already waiting under the oak tree.

They took their positions and started their ten deep breaths as if they were in a hurry. And we helped them pass out again. Only this time we felt them up, like Georgie-Porgie said, rushing to get in as many feels as we could before they came back from not knowing where they were. We looked at each other the whole time across the twilight, but couldn't really see each other's eyes.

Georgie-Porgie signaled when it was time to stop, making a hatchet motion with his arm. And we moved our hands behind our backs until the girls woke up.

Marla Hawkins's head remained on my thighs for a while, and then she rolled to the side and her face hit the grass. She looked up as if she didn't know who I was, which made me wish it was completely dark out so I wouldn't have to see her. Because I felt bad, even if I only did what Georgie-Porgie said she wanted.

Sin multiplies the more you are aware of it and do nothing, Father Larkin said. But I couldn't tell him about Marla Hawkins, because he would know it was me through the black screen. So I would have to find another priest in another church somewhere, and then I could confess.

But what if I thought about it again afterwards? Would the sin return? And if sin could repeat in the memory, then confession was no good. And memory wasn't, either—where you can enjoy things over and over. Like remembering about feeling up Marla Hawkins as she lay asleep and not pretending, with the strange rush of blood from my stomach I had never felt before, taking me to a place I had never been, where you can't stop the rushing once it begins as your body burns from the inside out.

The third time the girls wanted to do it to us. Taddy Keegan didn't care, because he wanted to pass out. "Like going on a trip somewhere," he said. But Georgie-Porgie and I didn't want to, and I didn't think it would work anyway.

So I focused on faking it when Marla Hawkins squeezed me with all her might, her breasts and shoulders pressing into my back in a way that felt good, if I could just hang on . . .

At the final moment, her perfume hair fell around my neck, confusing it all until I started worrying if my shirt smelled clean, not like Taddy Keegan's, which smelled like melted cheese because he wore it too long. My mother told me one time, "Poor Mrs. Keegan has to do laundry for nine children. Ten, if you count Mr. Keegan."

And then I was gone . . . and couldn't worry anymore about cheese hair or bike grease or dinner left on hands that didn't smell like girl hands. Because the blackness came at me, just like Taddy Keegan said, and then the warm rush out of it, from the stomach up, feeling a lot like when Marla Hawkins backed herself into me, or when I was trying to feel her up through her gray sweatshirt.

And the coming-back feeling . . . as if your body isn't your body, but trying to control it anyway. And trying to remember—this is where I was before . . . And unable to remember if she touched me like I touched her, but imagining her hand there, and that's why it feels numb. And that's why it's better to be touched when you're not passed out, so you can remember what it's really like.

I wanted to ask Taddy Keegan if the girls did anything to us. But he would've just shrugged. And I couldn't ask Georgie-Porgie, because he was too big to have really passed out.

And it didn't matter anyway—not after Marla Hawkins drew me back inside her black sweater beyond the static electricity, inside the soft smelling where the dreaming sense takes over.

When I finally stood up, sort of wobbly in the darkness, I heard Georgie-Porgie yell from across the shadows, "Wasn't that amazing?!"

Taddy and I didn't say a word, because we knew he was lying.

⋏⋏⋏⋏⋏⋏

Marla Hawkins stopped by my front yard on her bicycle the next day to tell me everyone was meeting at her house that night, since her parents were away at their cabin in Ligonier. So after dinner, I went up to Mohawk Drive and knocked on her door just as it was getting dark. The curtains were still open and I could see the empty living room.

She opened the door and we sat on the couch at opposite ends.

"Where is everyone?" I finally asked.

"I don't know. I told them all to come."

More minutes passed and no one showed up. And I began to feel nervous about being in her house alone, even though I liked the fact that no one knew where I was, especially Taddy and Georgie-Porgie, who were probably right across the street under the tree.

I wanted to leave, but didn't want to miss a chance to do something with Marla when we weren't passed out. Maybe she felt the same way, because she shifted across the couch in her white long-sleeved shirt, like the kind my father wore.

We kissed, but it didn't last long, because she threw herself backwards across the couch with her arms flung to her sides like a rag doll. She gestured for me to come down on top of her, but I felt scared, my heart pressing through my skin.

I bent over to kiss her again, but she didn't seem to want that, and instead put my hand on her breast. Then she started breathing heavy, like under the oak tree, only faster. I could feel her breath against my face and her chest heaving up through her shirt, making me wonder if something was wrong with her.

She moved my hand to her shirt buttons and helped me until I could see her bare body in the dim light, and the rounds of her breasts pressing tight against her white bra. Her eyes remained closed, and her perfume was everywhere as she started moaning.

"Are you OK?" I asked.

"Don't stop," she said, with her chest heaving at me and her breath mixing into her perfume.

She placed my hands back on her breasts, and I squeezed them through her bra. But that made her breathing worse, so I stopped. She pressed my hands again.

"Are you sure you're all right? Are you sick or something?"

She didn't answer, but opened her eyes like she was angry, and then closed them in a dreaming way.

I unbuttoned the rest of her shirt and put my head down on her chest like we had done under the tree when she had her sweater on. But she pushed me off and began twisting her body from side to side and arching her back as if she were trying to get out of her bra without hands, or as if she were in pain.

Maybe she's trying to pass herself out, I thought, *without me squeezing her.*

I fiddled with the front of her bra, but my hands were too excited and my lower body was moving against her in a way I wasn't controlling. When I tried reaching around her back, my cheek landed next to hers. So I started kissing her there and forgot about the bra. And that's when she suddenly sat up and opened her eyes.

"Let's go upstairs to my bedroom," she said, out of breath.

Everything stopped inside me, the body excitement passing away until I was back into the nervousness again.

In the bedroom, she will take off her clothes and then I will have to take off mine. And then . . .

But Katy Casady would be different. We'd be hugging with clothes on, without breathing.

She was up on her elbows and staring at me in the darkened living room, her white shirt draping off the couch. I tried putting my hand back on her breast but she moved it away.

"Let's go upstairs," she said again. "Don't worry. When my older sister gets home, she'll do the same thing."

She stood and moved toward the steps. But I stayed on the couch, feeling a heaviness inside. I knew I wasn't going upstairs. And I couldn't walk out the front door, either, because Taddy Keegan and Georgie-Porgie would see me from across the street.

"I've got to go," I announced loudly, as if there were a group of people in the room.

"You can't leave me like this," she said in a serious way.

There was light coming from a streetlamp on Mohawk because the curtains were still opened—and I could see her white bra inside her open shirt. I wanted to see what she looked like without it, but I had to go up to the bedroom for that. And I could see her eyes staring into me, even though her face and hair blended into the darkness.

I knew about Marla Hawkins's back porch from all the times I cut through the backyards. I was prince of the backyards. I knew who had a dog and who didn't, and who had a badminton net or a patio, or who had an elevated back porch.

I turned and opened the porch door. There was a thin white curtain in front of it. After closing the door, I could see her gauzy through the glass—still standing, eyes completely opened and shirt unbuttoned, as if she still couldn't believe I wasn't going upstairs with her.

I wanted to say sorry, but she wouldn't have heard me through the glass. And I felt like I didn't have much time. But I should have slowed down enough to hang from the porch railing before letting go, rather than jumping from the top of the rail, falling about ten feet into the darkness, thinking in that second how I'd lost all chance of touching Marla Hawkins again, and of seeing her without clothes.

I hit the ground hard, my knee banging into my chin, driving a headache up from my teeth, and my ankle twisting just a bit as I rolled against the wood trellis under the porch.

I got up and ran, and didn't know why, and worried about tripping over things in the blind backyards, with the nervousness still inside me and my ankle not feeling right, and the sweat from the warm July air and her house with all the windows closed, which is why I didn't smell the rain coming.

A few minutes later, I forced my way between the diseased poplar trees at the top of our yard. I planned on going through the kitchen door and past my father, who would be pacing back and forth in the living room. He would just look up and not say anything. But as I stepped onto the lower backyard, I saw an orange glow coming from the porch and knew my sister was there. Then I heard my mother's voice calling me.

"Yes?" I said.

She was having her nightly beer and waiting for the rain, because she loved listening to it on the porch roof.

"Where are you coming from?" my sister asked.

I wanted to act normal so she wouldn't think there was anything different about me, but normal didn't seem to be there.

After a few more steps, I stopped by the back door. I could hear the quietness between the crickets inside the thickening smell of rain, and I watched the moving glow of my sister's cigarette as she took another puff, the stream of smoke almost visible.

"I have to use the bathroom," I said.

I really wanted to go sit with my mother and sister, as long as they didn't ask questions. But Marla Hawkins kept getting in the way, lying underneath me with her shirt wide open.

The house was warm and smelled like Lestoil, because it was Lorraine's cleaning day. I waited until I got to the third floor before taking my shirt off—my mother didn't like men going without a shirt around the house. Then I laid on the bed and turned off the lamp so they would think I was going to sleep, and tried to keep real still so the bed springs wouldn't creak.

I didn't go to Marla Hawkins's bedroom because I was afraid of what she wanted, because she would take her clothes off and then I would have to . . . like my cousin when we were four, under a small tree at the side of her backyard with my mother and aunt sitting below on the back porch drinking iced tea, because it was a hot, humid afternoon . . . my cousin saying she was going to show herself to me and I said you'd better not, but she did it anyway, and then I had to show myself back at her, which I didn't want to do, the whole time hearing my mother's voice echoing against the brick house. They couldn't see us because of the porch awning, but we could see their feet—my aunt's right shoe dangling loose as her leg rocked back and forth in the still heat.

After that, my cousin always looked at me in a way that felt uncomfortable. Like she was saying with her eyes: *We really did show ourselves that time, under the tree. Don't you remember?*

The rain finally arrived, coming down hard like it does after waiting too long. On the third floor roof, the noise was so loud it drowned out everything. I knew I should close the windows so the rain wouldn't blow through the screens. But I liked the damp breeze across my body and couldn't make myself get up.

I thought about my mother sitting below under the yellow corrugated porch roof, enjoying the sound of the rain, and how nice it would be to sit with her, especially since my sister had probably gone out and left her there alone. "Listen to that rain!" my mother would say to me. "Do you believe it?" Like the rain was a miracle.

And it was falling hard on Taddy Keegan and Georgie-Porgie under the oak tree, making them go home sooner than they wanted.

And Marla Hawkins, in her dark house hearing the rain against the living room windows, but not enjoying it because she was still angry at the boy who jumped off her back porch and ran away . . . making me wish I could be sudden-asleep so I wouldn't have to think about Marla Hawkins anymore. Like passing out under the oak tree, and drifting back to where I was before ever going inside her house.

But there was too much nervousness inside my body to sleep, especially with the rain batting hard on our slate roof and worrying about the water blowing in through the screens, and with my ankle still throbbing.

Maybe the rain will last forever . . . *until it's just me and my third-floor bedroom existing away. And I'll drink rainwater to live, like drops from the ravens. Until it's time to lie down and wait for the eternal sleep darkness to roll in . . .*

Because Taddy Keegan was right. All we want is to wake up and not know where we are. But it only lasts for a little while, which isn't enough.

Dulaney's Cave

Mr. Schiezer wore white short-sleeve shirts that seemed too small for him, and thin, dark ties. His large-frame glasses blocked his face, so you couldn't quite see what he looked like, and you never wanted to look long enough to find out.

In seventh grade, he was our science teacher again, and also our basketball coach. Sometimes, he'd take a few of his favorite players down to the caves near Uniontown, where they would hike to see stalactites and stalagmites. The place was called Dulaney's Cave, and I always wanted to go there.

At more than two miles, Dulaney's Cave was known as the longest natural underground tunnel in Pennsylvania. And most of the cave was in absolute darkness, so twilight never had a chance of coming on. Its cliffs were twenty to sixty feet high, and the damp air always fifty-two degrees, because there was no weather in Dulaney's Cave—no summer and no winter. But Mr. Schiezer never mentioned that. He just talked about the darkness.

"Have you ever seen absolute darkness?" he asked us in class one day. "Of course not. There is no absolute darkness in our world. Only in the caves. And it is more real than anything you can imagine."

He talked as if he was sad about it, while pacing in front of the chalkboard with his head down, his combed-back hair falling forward.

"You're not going to find absolute darkness in your basement, or under your bed covers. So you can forget about that," he said, gesturing dismissively with his hands.

And I thought, *Yes, he's right. Because no matter how carefully I hide under the sheets, the vague light always finds a way in after a while.*

And that's why I wanted to see absolute darkness, which didn't make any sense. How could I actually see something that means you can't see anything? . . . *waiting for your eyes to adjust and nothing happens, like in the sewer tunnel with Taddy Keegan, imagining light in a recess somewhere that doesn't exist, because the idea of eternal darkness is too much, even though Sister Lorraine says God resides inside darkness, too.*

I wanted to see stalactites and stalagmites for real, not just pictures in a book. Because I couldn't believe dripping water could shape rock that way. Flowstone, Mr. Schiezer called it—especially the upward ones, formed from cave rocks dripping downward for thousands of years. Gravity can do strange things with limestone, until, after a while, an underground river flows. But who can row a boat through a cave?

Mr. Schiezer said there was no river. And that's why you have to spelunk your way through Dulaney's Cave, walking on soil that is brownish gray—*fuscous*, he called it.

But I would never go with Mr. Schiezer, even if he asked, because I wouldn't take the chance of "being mo'd by him," as Big Mori said, even though I wasn't quite sure what that meant . . . in a place where the light never comes on no matter how long you wait.

When I asked some of the basketball players why they went to

Dulaney's Cave if they knew Mr. Schiezer would try to mo them, they said it wasn't a big deal. They just pushed him away and he would stop. So I guess it was worth it for them in order to see the stalactites.

And Mr. Schiezer knew that I knew, and that's why I never got invited, and why he never played me in the seventh grade basketball games. So I sat on the bench, watching Billy Creely and the others out there, with everyone thinking I was too skinny to play, or just not good enough, with Mr. Schiezer waiting for me to quit. But he didn't know about my mother, who told me never to quit anything.

And I told her she couldn't go to the games, because I didn't want her to see me on the bench, hating the coldness inside the strange auditoriums, with their sad fluorescent lights and wearing the thin purple uniform that didn't cover my shoulders and made my body look skinnier, with the freezing metal chairs pressing through my shorts and bare skin, because I was just "pants with nothing in them."

Sometimes I would space out and forget where I was. And that's when Mr. Schiezer would call out my name, as if it were suddenly important for me to play in the last few minutes when we were losing by too many points to ever win. I guess he was tired of seeing me hunched over the chair breathing on the tops of my legs to keep them warm.

And then yelling at me out on the floor because I didn't know what to do, with the nervousness taking over so that the last thing I wanted was to touch the ball, and actually praying for that not to happen. But at the last second, it would be there: the sudden hardness of it in my cold fingers and the moist smell of rubber from all the other hands that had touched it. And all the arms grabbing at me at once, and everyone watching and thinking, *Mr. Schiezer was right. That boy can't play.*

Afterwards, I'd walk into the freezing autumn darkness wearing only my uniform under my coat and sit on the cold seats in Mr.

Nevin's car that never warmed up until we were driving down my street, and then it was too late.

But I still wouldn't quit, because I didn't want to disappoint my mother. Like when I was ten years old and spent so much nervous time memorizing the Latin Mass so I could serve as an altar boy—having to know by heart the Latin responses on both sides of the server's card sealed in plastic, and when to ring the bell three times, or carry the cruet and pour the water over Father Larkin's fingers while he spoke, "Lavabo inter innocentes manus meas"—"I will wash my hands among the innocent," and waiting for him to dry his hands and drape the damp white towel across my arm. And then carefully lifting his cassock over his shoes while staring at the soles, because they never seemed as clean as they should have been, as he knelt to pray with his back to the people.

My father told me to carry the Latin card with me wherever I went so that I could memorize in every spare moment, promising that if I learned it well, I could serve with the bishop at Saint Paul Cathedral. Bishop Wright was my father's friend. He even came to dinner one Sunday—a towering man, over three hundred pounds in a black cassock buttoned up tight under his fleshy neck. The closest man to the Holy Him, with drinks of bourbon and too many rings on one hand that touched our heads to give us his blessing as we knelt in the living room, making the sign of the cross with faces bent over and our dog, Vicki, barking because she never liked anyone in uniform. But that didn't matter, because my father always said that, if you have priests for your friends, you don't need anyone else. Which was all right for him, because he just paced alone every night, with bourbons on the mantle and a cigarette in hand.

"You're going to learn your Latin, aren't you, son?" my father asked in front of the bishop. "And then you can serve Mass at the Cathedral, and we'll all go. Wouldn't you like that?"

My father's words, like the Latin itself, were too much to take in.

But I kept memorizing the card, taking longer than I should have. And just when I finally knew it all, the Mass changed to English, because all the cardinals in Rome at Vatican II said so.

But it didn't matter if it was Rome or Pittsburgh, because I would never get my chance to recite the Latin for him at the Cathedral— Bishop Wright, who touched our soft heads in the living room while we knelt with eyes closed, before he departed.

So I told Father Larkin that I quit, because I had learned the Latin for nothing. And he said I could still think in Latin while reciting English, and that God would like that. *But anyone can do it in English*, I thought.

So Father Larkin made me join the choirboys instead. And then I had to quit that, too, because of the pollywogs . . .

Friday after school, I dropped the pollywogs in the holy water basin to see if they would act differently than those in creek water, which had to be a good science experiment, unless someone had tested it already and found out that holy water wasn't that special after all, which is why you have to just believe that it is. But I never got to find out, because on Saturday night, after I walked all the way up there, past the Big Intersection and up Washington Hill and down Fort Couch, it all turned out to be for nothing because the church doors were locked and I wouldn't be able to get my pollywogs until Sunday morning Mass, with everyone dipping their fingers to anoint themselves in Latin as they arrived, touching the holy water for just a second like it was on fire, and then dripping the water on the front of their clothes as they crossed themselves, and dripping more holy water on the church floor, even though something blessed should never spill.

Nothing holy could ever be destroyed, the nuns said, like communion hosts, even if they were vomited up, which is why the priests were the only ones who could handle it after it happened, maybe storing it in the sacristy inside a special chalice for vomited-up communion.

I wished I could ask Father Larkin about it, but he was too mad after the pollywogs to ask him about anything. And all because they locked the church on Saturday night, which meant that, if someone needed emergency praying, he would have to wait until Sunday morning, when the crowds at Mass would say the same thing in English at the same time, until you could hardly hear yourself think.

And that's why Father Larkin was right—saying Mass in Latin in your head was better. So I told my mother that I didn't want to go to Mass anymore, especially when Mr. Devine played his folk guitar, and that I would visit the church at night when no one was around, if I could just find a key. And she said, "What about communion and confession? Because you don't want to be in a state of sin in God's eyes."

⋏⋏⋏⋏⋏

In January, the ski trips with Buddy Nevin began. I had never skied before, but Buddy's father, known as "The Big B," got us free passes and lessons at Seven Springs, because he had a new job there. "He's in sales," Buddy said, raising one side of his face as he spoke.

When Buddy and I would come into the lodge to warm up, we'd see the Big B working on his sales at the bar. "This is my son, Buddy," he'd say to his friends. And they'd shake Buddy's hand and pat him on the shoulder.

Big B would pick me up in his gold Ford Galaxie with the black vinyl top on Saturday mornings when it was still dark outside. No one in the car said much, which was OK with me, because I was tired and didn't feel like talking.

The AM radio played low, with sports information and weather, and the heat was on high, making the car sickly warm. But I couldn't take my coat off, because I was stuck tight, shouldered between Buddy and his dad on the front seat, even though the back seat was open. "You can't sit in the back," Buddy said, "because Big B doesn't like to feel he's chauffeuring people around."

The cigarette smoke was thick, because Big B wouldn't open his window, and the windshield was so fogged up I wondered how Big B could see. That's why my father always opened the window when he smoked, and didn't care about the cold draft. And the hot ash would blow back and hit me and my sister in the face in the back seat.

In Big B's car, the smoke and heat made me sleepy. But I was afraid to close my eyes, because I didn't want Buddy and his dad to think I wasn't having a good time . . . Big B driving with the lights still on, even though the morning darkness was gone, and Big B concentrating because his car kept swerving on the ice-black road, his face and body close inside the strangeness that seemed to settle over us in the front seat, as if we were in a separate place that had nothing to do with where we lived, and nothing to do with where we were going. We were just on our way—me and Buddy and The Big B.

It made me wonder who I was when I was sitting there, and why the boy next to me was Buddy Nevin. But I already knew the answer to that, from back in fourth grade, on the playground after school, waiting in the early twilight for the late buses to take us home. Some of the kids were calling Buddy Nevin "Fatso," so after a while, I tried it, too, even though I didn't know him, and even though the word didn't feel right, because there were no other words before or after it—just "Fatso."

And Buddy said, "If you call me Fatso again, I'm gonna punch you in the mouth."

But I hardly paid attention, because I was already figuring how to say it again, in a safer way. I waited until I got on the school bus the last day before Christmas vacation, then pulled down the window and yelled, into the cold dusk, "Fatso!," as loud as I could so everyone could hear, and Buddy gazed up to find my face and looked disappointed in me.

On the first day back in mid-January, I heard voices circling around at recess in the freezing air: *Buddy Nevin is looking for you.*

So I guessed he did remember. But I still didn't want to believe it. Until I saw Buddy Nevin pushing through the kids on the parking lot as if they were tree branches, making his way toward me, his body tilting back and forth as his legs moved slow and patient inside the tight bottom of his winter coat, and his head covered with a black Steelers tussle cap pulled down to his thick eyebrows.

So I ran, which was easy. And every time he got close, I sprinted away again, with the other kids' bodies swirling in patterns on the asphalt as I passed, their heads turning at the last second.

Eventually, I must have tired Buddy out, because I couldn't see him anymore. So I stopped to catch my breath by the railing where the buses parked. And that's when I started feeling bad. Because even though I outran him, I still shouldn't have called him "Fatso," especially if he was going to remember it four weeks later. What did it matter, anyway, if Buddy Nevin was fat?

I turned to look at the little mountains of snow that the plow had dumped on the other side of the railing and wondered why we couldn't play there. For a few seconds, I watched my breath steam into the frigid air, and then I felt a gloved hand press hard on the back of my neck. I didn't think it could be Buddy, but when I turned around he was already pinning me against the railing, so there was nowhere to go.

Behind him, I saw the other kids' faces, but not their bodies, floating up against the white sky. Some looked serious, as if they were watching a nature experiment. Others looked ready to laugh.

The bell rang, signaling recess was over, and I thought that would be the end of it, because it was time to go back to Mrs. Malloy's classroom. But no one moved.

Buddy Nevin had his left hand under my chin; his right hand he put to his mouth, tugging his black leather glove off with his teeth so slowly that he had to breathe through his nose, and I could see the steam funnel out of his nostrils.

Finally, the glove dropped from his lips and fell across his jacket before hitting the ground soundlessly. *Why did he take his glove off?* I wondered. Because if I was going to hit someone, I'd want my glove on so I wouldn't hurt my hand. But Buddy Nevin had probably already thought about that as he stared, narrow-eyed, and never said a word, puffing through his mouth like he was short of breath. *He's just taking in extra air*, I thought, *preparing himself.* His warm breath smelled like wet straw, he was so close.

He took a step back, still holding onto my chin with his left hand. *This is my last chance to break away*, I thought. But I felt caught inside what he must have wanted to do for four long weeks.

Someone yelled "uppercut!" as if they could see his arm move before I could. And in the same second, I saw my own face from outside my body, yelling Fatso again through the bus window, and then I was back against the rail before the snowplow mountains . . . and then away again, with their faces looking down at me and Buddy Nevin taking his hat off and rubbing his crew cut, his eyes squinty, like he was trying to remember who I was.

A moment later, his face, and all the others, were gone. And Mrs. Malloy was there, telling me not to worry about the blood, and talking about my mother, who had already called the dentist, she said, because it was a permanent tooth.

And I didn't have to worry about the words that couldn't come out, or about crying, because there was nothing left to control. And I didn't have to talk to my mother in the car, because the bag of ice was over my mouth. And I didn't have to talk to Dr. Johnson or worry about the Novocain needle too big for his hand, and the smell of medicine and ammonia mixed together—or Dr. Johnson walking to the window afterward, as he always did, putting his foot up on the ledge and lighting his cigarette with his back to me, smoking in that position for seven minutes, because he knew it took exactly seven minutes for the Novocain to work.

The careful timing of one cigarette equaled the numbness smoked by one dentist reflected inside a window, seeing only his hands and the back of his head, and the stream of smoke that I wanted to last forever so the drilling couldn't begin, like little pins inside someone else's mouth that was really my mouth, saying *I'm all right* the whole time with words only I could hear, watching the cigarette fire up orange closer to his fingers, and his smoke blowing nostrils like steam coming out of two trains, because he was enjoying it so much.

Then, just like that, Dr. Johnson's cigarette time would end. He'd tamp the butt into his gold ashtray on the windowsill with a jerky motion of his hand, and then turn toward me, never looking in my eyes through his glasses, as if that would embarrass him somehow, or as if he was sad about something I couldn't understand.

After dinner that night, there was a knock at the door. My mother turned on the yellow porch light to see, but I already knew it was Buddy Nevin and his dad, even though I couldn't imagine them in our house.

They stood on the orange-green swirling carpet in our dining room, Mr. Nevin never taking his coat off, and my father never asking him to sit down—my father's face tilted the whole time into a painful expression, and he kept adjusting his glasses, even though he hardly looked at Mr. Nevin. My father seemed more bothered that his nightly routine of pacing had been interrupted than about this man's son punching his son.

Mr. Nevin turned his eyes toward Buddy, who was staring through the dining room wall like he wished he was somewhere else.

"I want to apologize for my son, Buddy," Mr. Nevin finally said. "But Buddy was only following what I told him to do. I said, the next time someone calls you *Fatso*, Buddy, punch him in the mouth."

And I couldn't help thinking how nice it would be if my father had told me something like that: "Son, if anyone ever calls you *Skinny*, punch him in the mouth."

"Your explanation," my father replied, in his lawyer's voice, "doesn't excuse your son."

"Would anyone like tea or coffee?" my mother asked.

"My son Buddy is a good boy," Mr. Nevin continued, as if he hadn't heard my father or my mother.

And I wasn't sure my father was hearing Mr. Nevin, which is why I wanted to yell, "Father, I did it! I called Buddy Nevin *Fatso!*"

But my father would only have shaken his head, his eyes down. Because he never said anything to me unless he had to. And when he did, he'd call me "son," even if I'd spent the whole afternoon with him. Like when we'd go to the Steelers games at Pitt Stadium, never saying a word as we drove in or while we walked up the hill after parking the car, past Mount Mercy College, where my older sister studied nursing, and through the "bad neighborhood," as my father called the Hill District where the Negroes lived, sometimes calling them niggers when he talked to Uncle Stanley if he thought I couldn't hear.

And then we'd sit down in the seats he'd had since the league started in 1933, with him telling me to buy three hotdogs just before halftime to avoid the crowd, and we'd have one and a half each, with nothing to drink because he didn't think of that. And he had his flask anyway, which he took from his inside pocket whenever he thought I couldn't see.

I wanted to go into the living room and play something with Buddy Nevin, and not watch my father and Mr. Nevin anymore. Because he was making Buddy's dad feel bad just by standing there, which is why The Big B would ask me to go skiing a couple years later, driving back home in pitch darkness down the Laurel Mountains towards Pittsburgh, the inside of the car smelling different than the morning, because The Big B had been doing his job at the bar all day inside the lodge. Just like my father smelled when he used to bend over and kiss me goodnight, only stronger.

And The Big B would talk about so many things at once I couldn't follow, making the car sound different from the quiet of the morning, as if he thought there was another adult in the car listening to him, when there was only me and Buddy.

Maybe The Big B had figured things out while we were skiing all day and needed to talk out loud to remember, while at the same time having to keep his Ford Galaxie from swerving on the ice, with the headlights seeing things a second too late and The Big B's tires sometimes going off the road into the high snow bank, and then back onto the road again, like a toboggan. And Buddy and I not saying a word, because we figured this was the way everyone drove down the mountain.

The Big B's face was hard to see through the cigarette smoke and car darkness, except when an oncoming headlight passed through the windshield, and he would squint through his glasses, still talking on—about our basketball coach, calling him "that bastard Schiezer" who "can't coach worth a damn. And I'll be goddamned if I'm going to let him ruin your chances, Buddy."

I wondered how much Big B really knew about Mr. Schiezer, because Buddy never went on the trips to Dulaney's Cave. So Big B couldn't know about the boys learning to push Mr. Schiezer away . . . *like I wanted to do to the janitor one time after raising my hand in Sister Joseph's first grade class to be excused for the bathroom . . . standing there trying, and him coming through the door and standing behind me, asking if I needed help, and I couldn't say, so he moved closer . . . eventually I ran back to Sister Joseph's class and decided to use the stalls the next time, because I didn't want anyone coming up from behind, because I didn't know exactly how the basketball boys pushed Mr. Schiezer away, and I couldn't ask my father the way Buddy could ask the Big B, because my father spoke without words. And I know my father—with the pain always in his face and turn-away eyes with long fine lashes behind black glasses, and his slicked-back hair, and his dry mouth moving even though he wasn't talking because of nerves, and that's why he paced . . . But he did stop one time to talk crazy Irish with Taddy Keegan, right in our living room, my father using his actor's voice, reciting some line about "the great sad rump of the world."* He's making it up, *I thought*, just like Taddy Keegan makes things up. *And so I hoped I could use an actor's voice sometime, and then I could talk to my father.*

One late afternoon in February, while waiting for the last school bus home, Billy Creely came up to me.

"I'm going to Dulaney's Cave this weekend with Mr. Schiezer," he said. "He only invites the best players. Did you know that?"

"You're going spelunking with him?"

"Yeah. My first time."

I wasn't sure if Billy Creely knew how to push Mr. Schiezer away inside the cave, but I didn't want to tell him about it either.

"You shouldn't go," I just said.

"Why not? You're just jealous because he didn't ask you."

"It's not worth it," I said, "just to see stalactites."

The next week, I heard that Mr. Creely took off work one day at the steel mill to go banging on the rectory door, demanding to see Father Larkin. And after that, we never saw Mr. Schiezer again.

There was only one basketball game left, so it didn't matter that much, and other teachers covered his classes. Later on, Conor McHenry told me that the oldest Creely, Chris, found out what happened to Billy in the caves and told his dad. So I felt bad about not doing a better job warning Billy. Unless maybe I wanted it to happen, which was a sin. Because Sister Helen said if you know something bad is going to happen and do nothing to stop it, you are part of the sin, too.

Billy Creely didn't brag as much after that, and never said anything about seeing the stalactites and stalagmites. And no one talked about Dulaney's Cave anymore—until a few weeks later, when my mother asked if I wanted to go. She must have heard what happened to Billy when she volunteered at the rectory. But we never went to see Dulaney's Cave—named after a man who was just a caretaker for other people's horses, until they found the cave under his land. But that was a long time ago.

The new plan, my mother told me, was to call it Laurel Caverns, because that sounded better as a tourist attraction. Just like the English Mass would be better than the Latin Mass, because more people would go if they could understand what the priest was saying.

My brother claimed that our father had defended a criminal one time named Dulaney, who was a descendent of the original Dulaney. And that my father actually visited the cave when he was a boy . . . *with the air exactly fifty-two degrees, whether in my father's time or mine, only the flowstone was shorter because of the years not happening yet, but you'd have to use a microscope to measure that . . .*

. . . and I could talk to my father in a fake actor's voice just like Taddy Keegan, and he would tell me about it, if he would just stop pacing for a while . . . And I could see the stalactites through his eyes, with nothing else around, except the absolute darkness.

The Mayfair

That winter, my father met a man named Lou. He would come to our house after dinner, and they would drink tea and talk quietly in the kitchen. Sometimes I walked in, pretending to look for something in the refrigerator, so I could overhear. Lou was a different kind of man than my father, and different than the kind of man my father would have been friendly with back when he used to see people.

In our kitchen, with the yellow metal cabinets all around and red Formica countertop and yellow linoleum floor, Lou talked about deals he had heard of, while my father paced back and forth and smoked cigarettes. Lou's "deals" were ways of making big money fast, which is why he started talking about the Mayfair one day—a shopping mall to be built on Route 88 at the bend in the road just before the county park, where there were only a few stores and lots of open spaces. Indoor shopping, Lou said, was the way it was going to be in the future.

I heard about the Mayfair from my mother as well, who had to sign some papers so my father could borrow money against our house. And she didn't want to do it, because "Lou isn't even a businessman," she said. "He's only a contractor, so what does he know?"

And I guess my father didn't know, either, because he was only a lawyer.

"Lou just wants to use your father's connections and reputation," my mother said to me, sitting in her usual spot on the living room couch and doing crossword puzzles.

Meanwhile, Lou and my father talked louder in the kitchen.

"Imagine," Lou said, "a place where people shop, only it's all inside. And there'll be walkways and atriums. Maybe even a hundred stores. Architects have the plans drawn up; the developers want to put it right here in the south suburbs, where the neighborhoods are expanding. We just need someone like you to pull it all together. No one wants to shop downtown anymore, not with the way the city is changing, so we're gonna bring the stores to them, with free parking all around and the convenience of having every kind of place you need under one roof."

"I only want to make a buck," my father said. "That's all."

Because my father didn't really like being a lawyer, which I noticed every time I visited him at work downtown after going to see Uncle Ted, who was a doctor and my father's brother, for an allergy shot. From the receptionist's desk, I would see my father in the distance, pacing around his office in circles with huge piles of folders stacked on his desk and the dead sunlight streaking across the floor where his legs crossed through every time he passed by the window.

Maybe if my father could just "make a buck," I thought, he wouldn't have to worry anymore about going to the office every day, and then maybe he could stop being nervous all the time and pacing around.

When I asked him one time what we would do if he actually made a buck, he didn't answer. So I asked if we could buy a pool table with some of the money, but he just continued pacing across our living room with his head down, rubbing his fingers nervously back against the palms of his hands.

I told him we could put the ping-pong table away inside its wall slot, and then bring it out and place it on top of the pool table anytime we wanted to use it. But still, he didn't say anything. I just sat there as he paced a few more laps across our living room. A couple times he glanced over at me as he passed by, probably thinking, *He's not going to leave unless I say something. So I will have to say something.*

After a few more minutes, my father finally spoke: "We'll have to see, son. I have to make a buck first."

When Lent was nearly over, my father added a new line to the nightly rosary he would say with my mother as they knelt down next to my bed: "And let's say a prayer for Mayfair."

But God didn't listen. The Mayfair deal collapsed when someone else started building a shopping mall first. It was called South Hills Village—the biggest indoor mall between Philadelphia and Chicago, the advertisements said. And they were building it right across the street from my school. With the Mayfair deal over, I would occasionally hear my father mutter, as he paced across our living room floor, "I only wanted to make a buck. That's all."

Lou kept coming by, and my father kept listening to him. Only now they drank bourbon that my father stored with the rest of the booze in a little cabinet above the broom closet in our kitchen.

Lou never mentioned the money my father lost on Mayfair. "Because he didn't lose any himself," my mother said. "Because your father is so gullible . . . He just believes whatever anyone tells him. All on a handshake."

Still, I wondered why my father didn't complain to Lou about the money. But my mother had an answer for that, too: "Your father is afraid Lou might not tell him about some new way to make the money up."

Maybe then, I thought, *my father will finally make a buck.*

ᚼᚤᚨᚤᚨ

In August, Buddy Nevin convinced me to join the eighth grade football team.

"C'mon, you can do it," he said. "Don't worry about being good. We all play like jagoffs."

Except for Taddy Keegan, because I had seen him run with the ball. He was a miracle in leg and body—stiff-arming tacklers, high-stepping around them, and sometimes leaping right over their heads and hands like a circus performer. And laughing most of the time, as if he had no idea how good he was. If you tried to tell him, he didn't seem to hear, because your words came from the falling-down world that he didn't belong to. And that's how I finally understood that no one could ever really be friends with Taddy Keegan. You just watched him inside his Taddy Keegan world that you could never touch, like the tacklers could never touch him.

"I'm too skinny to play football," I told Buddy Nevin.

"What about Kevin Hauptman?" he said.

He was right. Kevin Hauptman, with his woodpecker blond hair, was almost as skinny as I was, and it didn't seem to bother him. So I picked the position of offensive end, because that was the position Kevin Hauptman played. The only problem was Billy Creely, the quarterback, who only threw passes to Kevin Hauptman and never to me, even if my play number was called.

After practice one hot afternoon, when Billy Creely had already left the cramped locker room that was really just a converted janitor's closet, I noticed his helmet resting upside-down and lonely in the middle of the concrete floor. Some of the boys were forming a circle around it and talking matter-of-factly about who was going to piss inside Creely's helmet first. They decided I was the one, because Billy Creely never passed to me. But I didn't want to do it.

"Go ahead," Frankie Lacosta demanded, his face red-looking in the hot sweat.

Moments passed, with them waiting—Frankie Lacosta and little Pinky Sedona and Dave Conley and Delucci and Kevin Hauptman, and even Ronny Leeds and Buddy Nevin. *There is no running away*, I thought. *They think I owe them because they turned against Creely for me. So I have to do it. I have to piss inside Billy Creely's helmet.*

So I tried, but nothing came out. As the eternal seconds pressed through me in the small room with no windows and the locked door, I thought I was going to pass out. Maybe my soul knew it was wrong, or the ghost got me.

"Move out of the way," little Pinky Sedona said. "We can't wait forever."

He pushed me, even though he didn't have to, since he had his own angle to piss from into the helmet.

"Don't get it on the floor!" someone yelled at him. "You have to keep it in the helmet."

They laughed while Pinky Sedona missed the helmet, because you never know how far it's going to shoot at first. Then Delucci pushed him and Pinky missed some more. And they laughed some more.

"Cut it out!" Frankie Lacosta yelled. "He's got to get it in the helmet before he runs out."

When he finished, the helmet had become a purple and gold bowl half-filled with urine. *Even Billy Creely doesn't deserve this*, I thought. So when we left, I made sure I was the last one out, and I kicked over the helmet before closing the door.

Everyone scattered in different directions, but I walked slowly because I didn't care about getting caught. I noticed the dusk coming on because we had lost track of time inside the locker room that had no windows.

The next day, Billy Creely tried not to cry when he found his helmet surrounded by a half-dried puddle of Pinky Sedona piss. But he didn't practice with us and Bobby Schultze, a seventh-grader, played quarterback instead.

When my mother came to pick me up, I told her I was getting a ride later with the Big B. And then I waited under a tree across the dirt football field until everyone was gone and the darkness started dropping around.

I knew the key was on the ledge above the locker room door where both coaches could get to it. I went in but was afraid to put the light on until I realized no one could see me once I closed the door.

Using the janitor's oversized sink, I washed out the helmet with some of the chemicals that were there, which made my hands burn. *That's OK,* I thought, *because I deserve it for what we did.* Most of them weren't even my friends, except for Buddy Nevin and Ronny Leeds, who had to know it was wrong, too.

When Billy Creely came to practice the next day, Bobby Schultz still played quarterback, and Billy was the back-up. And Bobby Schultz was cool, with his curly dark hair hanging over his eyes and never saying much. I wished I could be like him, the same way I used to wish I could be like Taddy Keegan.

At the game on Saturday, Bobby Schultz passed to me—slants and button hooks—that I caught, because I really was an offensive end, and because you don't have a choice when you turn around and the ball is already there . . . *so that you only have to worry about running, with time stopping and starting, and everyone trying to hit you at once, which would seem strange if you had time to think about it . . . inside the sunken wet rectangular field, surrounded by trees already bare, owned by someone else's church and someone else's school nowhere near your home, with the cloudy afternoon closing around you and the air itself feeling too tight to breathe, mixed with the thick smell of wet mud and dead leaves underneath the fading daylight because, in late October, the games really do finish in the dark, like*

Buddy Nevin said . . . and you can only escape for a few seconds by running before getting tackled, while the dusk hour passes through you from around the trees, filling you with the sad smell of fall itself, and the cool dampness pressing into your feet, because your shoes aren't real football shoes, so the wetness and mud always find a way in . . .

On November 1, All Saints' Day, our whole class had to go to confession because it was a holy day of obligation. I thought about confessing to Monsignor Rooney about Billy Creely's helmet, because I still felt bad about it every time I saw him wearing it, wondering if the dried piss was getting into his hair, because chemicals can't wipe away everything.

But as we shuffled into the pews inside our temporary aluminum church, I didn't feel like confessing—not about Billy Creely's helmet, and not about what Mr. Schiezer did to him in the cave, which was my fault, too. *They can make you walk to church,* I thought, *but no one can make you go to confession. And why should I tell my sins to some priest, even if he is a monsignor? Just one step below a bishop, but Rooney is still only a man, even if you should never refer to a priest by just his last name, my mother says, since it's disrespectful.*

And Monsignor Rooney didn't even enjoy being a priest. I could tell from watching him wince when he drank the communion wine from his chalice in front of the whole church, as if he was trying to force it down. Or when I used to see him drink inside the sacristy when mass wasn't going on, and wincing then, too.

Just like my father taking big gulps of his bourbon highballs before dinner and wincing as if he really didn't like the taste of it. But forcing it down anyway. Making me wonder why he didn't try some other booze he might enjoy more. But my father had to drink bourbon highballs, because that's what he had always drunk, wincing with each swallow before setting his glass back on the high stone mantle in our living room. And then alternating his L&M and Kools cigarettes, regular and menthol, and probably not even sure why he smoked those particular brands, except that it was the way he had always done it.

And pacing without talking as if he didn't see my mother and me sitting there. My mother on the couch doing her crossword puzzles and me wishing I was up in my third-floor bedroom until the call for dinner, which had to be meat, potatoes, and vegetable, or else my father wouldn't eat. Like the time my mother tried serving lasagna and he just sat there, with his hands posed on either side of his plate, until she took the lasagna away and cooked him some pork chops along with instant mashed potatoes and canned peas. And even then, my father still wouldn't talk. So my mother and sister and I had to do all of that, while my father avoided looking at us and stared somewhere else—someplace empty and painful that we could never get to.

And that's how I knew the monsignor wasn't happy being a priest. Only he had no one to confess it to, except maybe himself while looking in a mirror, his creased face tilting downward and his eyes hard to see behind his long lashes and thick, crooked glasses.

When Monsignor Rooney did come to Sunday dinner, it was because my mother invited him. My father practically ignored him because Monsignor Rooney wasn't a Jesuit. And it was too bad, because Rooney and my father could have enjoyed each other's company, not-talking together, wincing while they drank booze they didn't like, and smoking cigarettes they believed would somehow make them feel better.

Meanwhile, my decision not to go to confession weighed upon me, especially when something else happened—the Saturday evening after our last football game of the season, when we walked by the nearly completed new octagonal St. Thomas More Church and saw Mr. Devine's car. Little Pinky Sedona reached through the partially open window and fed Mr. Devine's cat a pill he stole from his older brother that he said was LSD. None of us was sure what LSD was, and none of us believed Pinky, until we heard the next day about Mr. Devine's cat jumping off the aluminum church roof and not landing on his feet, like cats always do. When Mr. Devine came out, after practicing his folk guitar for Sunday Mass, he found his cat lying dead on the pavement.

Frankie Lacosta made us promise not to tell anyone. But I would have liked to confess it to a priest. Because you can say things to them, and they can never tell anyone.

ᛉᛁᛉᛁ

In early December, a new girl joined our eighth grade classroom. Her name was Patty Hasty. Mr. Devine said something about her father having been transferred to Pittsburgh, so she didn't have any friends. I wanted to be Patty Hasty's friend, but was afraid because she was too pretty, with her half-blond hair that waved over her perfect shoulders and green eyes that stopped right at you.

Buddy Nevin said Patty Hasty was a bitch. But I didn't believe him, because I felt the sex for her every time she was near. So when Buddy dared me to prove him wrong, I decided to ask Patty Hasty if she wanted to meet me sometime.

"How about at Horne's?" she said, as if Horne's department store would be an exciting place to go, whereas for me, it was just a place inside the new mall that had prevented my father from making a buck.

Her face got close as she continued: "My mother's taking me shopping at the new mall on Saturday. So I could meet you there, at Horne's."

I didn't say anything, because I wanted to talk with Georgie-Porgie first. He probably knew all about how to meet girls inside a mall. But when he told me I should meet her at the elevator, I wasn't so sure. Because it would just be me and her inside the closing doors.

"That's the whole idea!" Georgie snapped, because he didn't have patience for anyone who disagreed with him. "The girl will like it," he said confidently. "Trust me."

When I told Patty Hasty about the elevator, she actually said, "That's perfect," which made me think I should never question Georgie-Porgie again.

"I can tell my mother I'm going to the lower level to look for something," she said excitedly. "And we can meet. How about 1 p.m.?"

For the next two days, I dreaded Saturday at 1 p.m., and tried not to think about it. But the Horne's elevator remained solid before my eyes, making me wonder why people agree to do things they can't look forward to.

Let Georgie-Porgie go instead, I thought, *because he knows all about the elevator plan. Or Buddy Nevin, because he could find out on his own if Patty Hasty is a bitch.*

On Saturday, I walked all the way to the mall from my house and, even though it was freezing outside, I was sweating inside my heavy coat before I reached Mitchell's Corner. "WELCOME TO THE GRAND OPENING OF SOUTH HILLS VILLAGE MALL," a sign said in the distance.

I took my coat off when I got inside Horne's because I didn't want to sweat when I met Patty Hasty, and I looked for a place to stash it. *Under a bed*, I thought, *because they always have bedroom displays in stores like this.*

So when no one was looking, I stuffed my coat under one of the large beds with too many pillows, and then headed to the elevator while going over Georgie-Porgie's instructions in my mind:

Make sure no one else is there, then move immediately inside the elevator. You must be alone in the elevator. If someone else is there, walk her around for a while pretending to be shopping for something. Then, once inside the elevator, concentrate on the panel of buttons. As soon as the doors close, hit the STOP button. You must do this right away in order for the elevator to actually stop between floors. Remember, don't hit the Emergency button, because that will sound the alarm. You want the STOP button. Then, don't wait even a second; start kissing her right away. Because you won't have much time. And that's what she expects. Otherwise, ipso facto, she would never have agreed to meet you at the elevator.

And I did exactly as Georgie-Porgie said. I even hit the right button, stopping the elevator between floors, which didn't seem to surprise her as she stood slightly smiling with her arms unfolding.

But I couldn't make myself move farther. My head and body felt frozen, just like the elevator. And I wondered what it would be like if I stayed like that forever, with the slow ticking seconds that you can actually hear even when there is no clock . . .

Patty Hasty moved instead and touched my hands. Then she pushed her lips hard at me, making my mouth open to her tongue in a way no one ever tells you about, not even Georgie-Porgie—and tasting her smell of lipstick as it passes into your nose like fine powder. Because how could Georgie-Porgie know the truth about a girl like Patty Hasty, who I didn't deserve to be kissing anyway? And no one tells you when to stop, and that's why I kept on for as long as she wanted. Patty Hasty, Patty Hasty . . .

Until the banging on the elevator door that must have been going on a while before I noticed it, and it made me stop even though I didn't think she wanted me to. Because I never wanted to disappoint Patty Hasty, especially in an elevator.

A man's voice sounded far off, even though I knew it wasn't: "Are you all right in there? Are you stuck?"

The elevator lurched upward as soon as I released the STOP button, and the timed moments started flowing again. The doors opened a second later, and there was a big man standing on the other side, his eyes glancing right past me and into Patty Hasty, as if he had never seen a girl like her before. Maybe that's why she said, "See you later," and walked out without even mentioning my name.

She disappeared behind the perfume counter, and I thought how Georgie-Porgie was right. Patty Hasty was only interested in the elevator. And I would never be able to go out with her like other boys go out with girls, and no one would ever say, "Hey, he's with Patty Hasty. Do you believe it?"

"See you Monday!" I yelled back, but she was already too far away to hear.

A week later, my memory of Patty Hasty in the elevator seemed unreal, especially since she was ignoring me at school. I doubted if I even put my coat under the bed at Horne's. So I went back to the mall the next Saturday at the same time to do it again, just to see if it felt familiar. And it did. And I kept circling past the elevator to see if she would somehow appear, but she never did.

I thought about writing Patty Hasty a letter to see if she wanted to spend some time with me again at Horne's. But I had waited too long and it just didn't feel right.

By January, Patty Hasty was gone after being in Pittsburgh only a month. Her father got transferred again, someone said. Unless maybe her father wasn't even real. Because it's hard to imagine Patty Hasty having a father.

The next time, Lou said, "It's an honest-to-goodness sure thing." But my father seemed to have his doubts. It was mid-November, and the new deal concerned Christmas trees, thousands of them on some property eighty miles north of Pittsburgh. "The land is peaking with the kind of fir trees people like to have in their homes at Christmas,"

Lou said. "Balsams and Scotch pines—we wouldn't buy the property, just the trees. And the owners are willing to part with them for under two dollars apiece. It's a steal."

So all Lou and my father had to do was cut them down, haul them to the Pittsburgh suburbs, and sell them for between eight and fifteen dollars. With over twenty thousand trees, and an average profit of ten dollars per tree, they would easily make enough to erase my father's debt and still make a buck.

My father was hesitant, though. He told Lou that success depended upon good transportation and reliable sellers. And Lou told my father just to buy the trees and deal with the banks, and he would take care of everything else. "At the low price we'll be buying the trees for," he said, "we'll be able to undersell everyone else. All the retailers will be banging on our door."

They planned a drive up north to an area just past Sheakleyville to examine the trees. And my mother asked if I could go along, though I wasn't sure why.

So Lou drove his truck with all three of us in the front seat, and we made stops at several properties, each time my father saying, "The trees look pretty damn good." And I agreed, even though I didn't have much to compare them with.

A few days later, my father made a deal with another bank, and within a week, the northern fir trees were suddenly our fir trees. Meanwhile, Lou talked to some delivery men and started contacting retailers.

The problem was time. By early December, the cheap price on the trees didn't matter, since there weren't enough days to get rid of them. Lou and my father also had no idea how many other people would be selling trees at the same time. By the second week of December, it was what Lou called a "buyer's market."

Almost fifteen thousand trees had been cut, and most were still lying on the hillsides up north. Before it was all over, my father ended up trying to sell some of the trees himself in a parking lot he rented from the new shopping mall across from my school.

In the late afternoons, I would walk over from St. Thomas More and help him sell the trees. My sister, too, would walk from the girl's Catholic high school about a mile away. Most of them were bought by neighbors and people from our parish, everyone looking surprised that a downtown lawyer was standing in the cold with frozen gloves and smoky breath selling Christmas trees.

Eventually, my mother, who stayed at home because she was embarrassed that her husband was trying to make a buck selling trees in a parking lot connected to the mall that had brought about his first investment disaster, insisted that my father rent a heater and tent to keep her children warm. But the strong smell of kerosene mixed with pine made it hard to breathe, and the outside cold felt better. And I didn't want to miss any chance to sell a tree, because I was the best salesman in my family—better than my older brother, who eventually came home from medical school to help, and better than my sisters and my father. I knew how to convince people to buy a tree once they looked at it, for whatever price I made up. Just by shivering a little bit while holding the tree, I could make them feel sorry for me, especially on the verge of Christmas.

If they wanted a Scotch pine, I told them that was the best choice. And if they wanted a balsam, I would say the same thing, which was actually the truth. because my father always said that balsams are the best trees because they have shorter needles and last longer. He argued about this every year with Uncle Stanley, as if it was really important. Uncle Stanley was a Scotch pine man because he believed they had perfect shape. But my father claimed you could keep a balsam up until Washington's birthday if you wanted, and he proved it one year.

By Christmas Eve, almost all of the trees in our lot were sold, but thousands of others still rotted in the snow-covered hills up north, which kind of ruined Christmas that year, especially when it came time to bring home a tree for ourselves. There wasn't much left to choose from and my father was disappointed because he always liked an eight-foot tree so the star on top would touch the living room ceiling. But nothing that tall looked very good. We had waited too long.

My brother got the idea of connecting two trees together with a brace—a good-looking top of one tree with a good-looking bottom of another.

"No one will even notice it," he said. "Not through all the ornaments and branches."

"It's silly to nail two trees together," my sister said. "Especially when we own thousands of them."

My father didn't care either way, as long as it was eight feet and a balsam.

I didn't want to watch as my brother tried to screw the top of one tree onto another. My father didn't, either, and he wandered off behind the wooden trellises we leaned the trees against in the lot. I followed, thinking I might see him taking a sip from his flask. But when I peeked around the corner, where some scrawny trees were still leaning in the graying light, my father wasn't using his flask at all. He was giving a speech, low-voiced but dramatic, as if an audience were listening.

A freezing wind was blowing in my eyes, so I kept rubbing them while watching my father speak as if he were a different person, with language that sounded like he were in a play, maybe from his college days, when my mother said he played Hamlet and Macbeth. She said he was so good that Broadway made him offers after graduating in 1931. But my father's father, who had worked as a country doctor riding his buggy through the woods of south Pittsburgh to take care of people who had hardly any money, told my father he couldn't go into acting because of the immoral lifestyle, which I didn't quite understand. He told my father to choose either medicine or the law, and my father chose law because my mother said he couldn't imagine examining other people's bodies.

Behind the trellises, in the freezing dusk light, he rose on his toes with hand-gesturing and head-tilting under his brown businessman's hat. His speech continued at just over a whisper, and his body moved from inside his heavy wool coat in a way I had never seen before, as if he were a younger man. He said something about a character named Gloucester who wanted to kiss the king's hand, but the king had to wipe it off first because it smelled of mortality. *Not of pine trees . . .*

After a while, I felt guilty watching him and turned back toward the tent. But I didn't want to watch my brother, either, with his tree-saw and hammer. So I just sat on a stump until my father walked by, looking as if nothing had happened behind the trellises. And maybe it hadn't, except it was too real for me to have imagined it. How many times, I wondered, had he secretly done this before? Maybe he did it in front of Taddy Keegan, or maybe behind the piles of folders in his office where no one could see.

He walked past my brother, who was wrestling with a tree between his legs, and then stopped to pull his cigarettes from his right coat pocket, the L&M side. I walked over and stood near him, wishing I could see his face. But it was hard with his collar up and black glasses and hat underneath the closing darkness.

That night, my brother finally got our tree up in the living room. But no one felt very good about it, because it really was two trees, even though it was hard to tell. The whole idea was too much for my mother, who refused to even look at it.

When Aunt Julie and Uncle Stanley came to visit Christmas Day, Uncle Stanley stood with his Bloody Mary in hand and talked, as he always did, about the things he owned and which brands were best, like his Ford Thunderbird being better than my father's Buick that "was no damn good." And my father, not arguing back, just tilted his watery eyes in a way that showed contempt until Uncle Stanley turned away. And that's when he looked at our tree. I glanced over to see the nervousness in my mother's face.

"What did you do here? Put two trees together?" he asked, laughing, his cigarette ash falling from his mouth onto the carpet.

As soon as they left, my mother announced that next year she was going to buy one of the new artificial Christmas trees. And my father said he wouldn't let her bring a plastic tree into our house.

Father Sanders came to dinner that night, even though no one really wanted him there on Christmas but my father. It's always better to be kind, my mother always said.

Father Sanders was a Jesuit and, for my father, that's all that mattered, because, in his mind, a Jesuit was the best kind of holy man. "They are the crème de la crème," he liked to say. When I asked him what he meant by that, he said, "They are the best-educated class of men in the world."

But Father Sanders didn't look like crème de la crème. He didn't even look like any of the Jesuits we had known, who all had gray hair and red faces and shaky thin hands that looked holy, and who told stories of faraway places and amazing people they had met. Father Sanders had thin, brown, uncombed hair that my sister said was always greasy, and skin that looked almost yellow, especially his face, which was marked with little holes in his cheeks. And none of us wanted to sit next to him at dinner, because all he did was smile as if something funny was going on that we didn't know anything about.

I had no idea how my father knew Father Sanders, especially since he lived on the other side of Pittsburgh and had no car. So when he came to dinner, we'd have to pick him up in the late afternoon and then drive him all the way back at night.

My older brother referred to Father Sanders as "the leech," but never in front of my father. And it upset my mother, who didn't like hearing an unkind word about any priest. My brother and sister would argue about who was going to have to drive Father Sanders back home, with my mother always worried Father Sanders might overhear.

I never trusted anything Father Sanders said, especially when he asked to excuse himself for twenty minutes before Christmas dinner to say his "office," a series of priestly daily prayers. With his drink in one hand and his little black book in the other, he headed upstairs and chose my sister's bedroom for the privacy. A few minutes later, I pretended to be looking for my sister and opened the bedroom door as if I didn't know he was in there. Next to the window, where my sister had her collection of Virgin Mary statues on a little table, Father Sanders lay on my sister's bed with his eyes closed and his drink balanced on his belly. Through the shadows, he turned to look at me for a moment with his short-lipped smile, and then turned back and closed his eyes again, his little black book still in his hand.

At dinner, my mother jumped up to refill his plate with more roast beef and potatoes and Le Sueur canned peas, and Father Sanders, sweating a little from his forehead, would pause every few seconds to push his glasses back up his nose before bending over to scoop up more food. And I kept thinking how unfair it was, because my mother told the rest of us, except for my father, to FHB—Family Hold Back, in case there wasn't enough food—and always to leave one bite on the plate so it didn't look like we were starving, especially when we ate at other people's houses. But Jesuits never get enough to eat, she said. And they're always cold, too, which is why she gave them sweaters at Christmas, the black kind that button up the front. Jesuits will never buy a sweater for themselves, she said.

But I didn't believe that, and wanted to sneak into Father Sanders' rectory sometime and look into his drawers. I bet he had dozens of sweaters stashed away. His problem was probably remembering which sweater was from my mother so he could wear it when he came to dinner. *One time, he's bound to mess up*, I thought, *and my mother will notice.*

After dinner was over, my mother took the wine bottle away so Father Sanders wouldn't get sleepy, because then he might want to stay overnight and she'd have to drive him back in the morning.

She stirred him from the table by asking for his blessing, and that's how we knew Father Sanders' Christmas visit was coming to an end. And she whispered in my ear, "Please ride along to keep your sister company when she drives Father Sanders home."

I couldn't say no, even though I didn't think my sister should have to go into the dark on Christmas night and drive across the city on streets my mother said were icy and poorly lit. But Father Sanders never seemed to think about that.

She whispered again, her breath warm on my cheek and without smell, asking me not to complain, because if Father overheard, he would want to take Father Sanders himself—and he could fall asleep behind the wheel, like when he ran into the telephone pole on Cochran Boulevard, or when he slammed into the front of our garage one night as he arrived home.

She gave me the *eyeball*, which meant I had to kneel down with everyone else to receive Father Sanders' blessing even though I didn't think his blessing would do any good because God probably wouldn't pay attention to him. And because I didn't want him to touch my head with his hands, or smile down at me with his yellow, tilted teeth. And I didn't want to kneel beneath his stained sweater and thin hair that he kept pushing across his forehead with square fingers, or glance upward at his shy eyes that looked away if you were steady enough to stare through him. And I couldn't imagine ever confessing to Father Sanders, or asking him to pray for special things, like when my father used to ask us to pray for the Mayfair.

When the blessing was over, my father stood up slowly, his knees creaking, and announced, "I'll take Father Sanders home." So my mother whispered a final time, without any breath at all, asking me to ride along to keep my father awake on the drive back, which was hard to do with a man who never talked to you, even if you kept asking questions, like, what are you going to do with the thousands of trees left on the ground up north? Or, do you think any fool can really see that our Christmas tree is just two trees nailed together, like Mother said?

And I wouldn't be able to see his face in the darkened car to know if he was actually listening, unless the approaching headlights streaked across for a second. And even then, with his head drooping like it always did, and his businessman's hat and thick black glasses, you couldn't see anything. But maybe I didn't want to see his face, because on that Christmas night, my father probably had the saddest face of all.

We made it safely back home in our old black Oldsmobile after taking Father Sanders across the city. And my father never spoke a word to me.

In the driveway, he turned off the engine and headlights. And then, for some reason, his body just seemed to stop, as if the winding key inside him had run down.

After a few moments, with him not moving in the cold stillness of our steep driveway, I felt afraid—not of my father, but of something beyond him that seemed to make him powerless in a way I had never seen before.

Both of his gloved hands remained on the steering wheel, like he was planning on driving the car without the engine on, maybe to a place you don't need an engine to get to. And I was afraid to open my car door, because he might not open his.

After a minute, he moved his hands and rested them on his thighs, which I thought was a good sign until I realized he was just settling into a more comfortable position. Again, I thought of opening my door to see what he would do. But if he didn't move, I couldn't leave him in the car alone. And if I asked, "Dad, aren't you coming?," he probably wouldn't answer. Or maybe he would just mumble, "In a minute, son." So no good would come of it.

More minutes passed, until I wondered if he had forgotten I was even there, or if maybe he was nodding off to sleep. But he always snored when he slept, and the car was quiet, except for the occasional ticking sound from the cooling engine.

My father was hunched over more than normal, sort of like he was trying to draw back inside himself. *What if he just wants to be alone for a while in the freezing car?* I thought. *And how could this be the same man who stood on his toes the night before, reciting Shakespeare on Christmas Eve behind a row of unsold trees in the new mall parking lot?*

I surveyed the other houses on our street to see if anyone might be looking out and wondering why my father was still inside his car. But the houses were all dark, except for ours, which had a single lamp on in the living room that my mother kept lit until the last person went to bed. The porch light was off, probably to save electricity. "People who leave lights on have more money than brains," she said.

Inside the stiffening darkness, I thought I heard my father sigh and say, "I only wanted to make a buck, son. That's all." But maybe I imagined it. And then I wasn't sure . . . especially since my father could talk without saying words.

I guess this is it, I thought. *We're just going to sit here in the Oldsmobile cold until we can't stand it anymore, except that the cold won't bother him as much.*

And then it didn't matter. Because my father said, without turning his head, "Let's go in, son." And just like that, it was over.

The Great Carnegie

In February, a month before turning fourteen, I started going to art classes on Saturday mornings at Carnegie Mellon Museum. I didn't want to go because it was too early to get up on a weekend, and because I had to ride there with Noni Donnely, a plain-looking girl whose first name was really Nora, and who did nothing but read books all the time.

They chose two eighth graders from every elementary school in Pittsburgh for the scholarship. And for St. Thomas More, it was me and Noni. Her mother and my mother were friends from volunteering at the library. So I was doomed to be with Nora Donnely, but I still didn't have to call her Noni. In fact, I didn't have to call her anything at all.

So when Mr. Donnely picked me up at 7 a.m., I didn't talk in the car. And it didn't seem to bother Mr. Donnely or Noni, who chattered on about Donnely things I couldn't follow while I leaned my head against the cold backseat window and tried to sleep. But every time their car hit a pothole or crossed a trolley track, I jerked awake and found myself staring into the gray dull morning with gray-white houses passing by in a steady stream. No people seemed to be moving at that hour on a Saturday, which made me wonder what I was doing in a strange car with the Donnelys anyway, a family who didn't even believe in record players or television.

"You can't quit," my mother said one Saturday morning.

Mr. Donnely's car was idling at the curb, the heavy white smoke piling out of the tailpipe into the frigid air.

"It's an honor to be invited," she continued. "You just have to stick it out."

"Whether I like it or not? Because I didn't ask to take art classes at the museum."

"Later on, you will see it differently," she said, her gray hair nodding at me and her hands moving nervously, because she was worried about keeping Mr. Donnely waiting.

"God gave you a gift, and if you don't use it, kiddo . . ."

Her voice sounded impatient, which was the only time she called me "kiddo."

"I would love to take art classes at Carnegie," she continued. "And any fool can quit."

I descended the three steps to our walkway and then turned back to see her face still peeking out from behind the heavy wooden front door. She waved to Mr. Donnely, who didn't seem to be looking at her through the foggy car window.

Her words made me think of Junior Achievement, and how she made me go to those awful meetings with Buddy Nevin. It was all Big B's idea, because he believed his own problem in life was never holding onto a job. He figured Junior Achievement would give his son Buddy a chance to learn the secrets of running a successful business.

But I hated Junior Achievement, and I hated the old, depressing building in Dormont where they held the three-hour meetings, and the old businessmen who pretended they wanted to help us become part of "the Economics of Life," making us repeat their mottos while we made up pretend companies that only a group of thirteen year olds would believe in.

So one night in Dormont, I didn't "stick it out." I just sat outside on the stoop the whole time until my mother picked me up and I told her I wasn't going back in there again.

"I don't want to be part of the Economics of Life," I said.

And for some reason, she didn't argue with me.

But she would never let me quit the art class, because it was at the great Carnegie Museum, so her pride was involved. But I don't think my mother understood how awful it was to be with Mr. Fornier, the art director, who wore his bowtie cheerfully at 8 a.m. as we sat in the cold, cavern-like amphitheater. And how he made us sing before class could begin.

I didn't want to sing. And I was hungry because of Mr. Donnely at 7 a.m. with no time to eat. And what did singing have to do with art, anyway, at the great Carnegie?

But Mr. Fornier's motto was "sing before you paint." "Singing makes you happy," he said. "And happy artists make good art." But it didn't make sense to me, because I figured lots of unhappy people made good art.

Mr. Fornier's voice squeaked at us through a microphone from the podium at the bottom of the art cave, so I could see only the top of his head and his bow tie, and never his face. Behind us, our easels were set up with fresh tubes of paint, as if we deserved to be there. But Mr. Fornier wanted us to sing first.

He chose a song from his favorite new musical, *Mame*, and made us sing it over and over until we were loud enough to make him happy, as we stood high above, lined along a dark wooden railing with paint smelling all around and the hollow-sounding music echoing from the small record player on the desk next to his podium below.

I didn't even know who Mame was, or why she made "the cotton easy to pick," or gave "the mint julep a kick." Or why she would make "the South revive again . . . Mame! Mame!"

But no one else seemed to care. Not Noni Donnely, who stood erect as if she were in church, her hands folded together and resting on the dark rail as though she were praying. She sang with her eyes closed, her thin brown hair falling back as she arched her neck like she was in a Fornier trance.

I was the only one who didn't sing.

A while later, the little Fornier man walked us down the long museum corridors of art until we stopped at a painting he liked. And then he told us to copy it in the "museum style" he taught us.

Noni never sat near me, so she wasn't a bother. And I actually would have liked to talk with her to help get through the four-hour class and the hunger from her father arriving in the smoking car too soon.

But talking to Noni wouldn't have worked, because she was too busy biting her thin lips as she concentrated on her painting, while the people visiting the museum walked by, looking at the great works on the wall, and then down at the eighth grade children and their lousy copies.

So I tried to keep them from seeing my painting, because I knew we were just eighth-graders pretending. But it was impossible to hide from so many passing in different directions, making me wonder why one kid didn't just stand up and paint right on top of one of the famous paintings on the museum wall. No one would get there in time to stop him, and then he would definitely get kicked out of the art class at the great Carnegie and wouldn't have to worry anymore about quitting.

〽〰〽〰

My father was supposed to pick me up at noon by the side door of the museum. But not Noni, whose father had to come all the way back in to get her, because we had a stop to make on the way home.

I hoped my father brought some lunch, but I knew he wouldn't. He didn't think of things like that.

He was late, as usual. So I stood inside where it was warm and stared through the glass doors. I thought I could see his black Oldsmobile in the parking lot, but without him in it. And then I wasn't sure. So I decided to go and check.

As I pushed through the doors, I noticed a group of Negro kids playing on the railings near the bottom of the wide stairs. They were trying to slide down the rail without falling off, and laughing about it. I wondered about them being there, because you never saw Negroes around the museum. *Maybe it's because of the rioting up in the Hill District*, I thought, *and these kids just wanted to get away.*

My father had told me that it started with "the niggers" throwing rocks down at the dome of the Civic Arena. And then my mother got mad at him for using that word. I also heard him say they would be coming into our neighborhoods eventually, carrying rocks and knives, even though we lived miles away. They would "sneak in at night," I heard my father say to a neighbor, "and we won't be able to see them."

I stopped to look at the boys for a second, and then I continued down the stairs, trying not to look at them any more because I didn't want them to think I was afraid of them.

I stared straight ahead toward the empty car. "Never show you're afraid," I remembered my mother saying—like in front of a strange dog. Just walk calmly away and ignore it. So that's what I tried to do, but I could feel the Negro kids watching me.

"Hey, what do you think we are, a bunch of monkeys?" one of them yelled.

"Yeah, he's lookin' at us like we're fuckin' monkeys!" another said.

"Hey, we're talkin' to you, kid. Don't you be walkin' on. You think you can stare at us?"

I kept walking as if they weren't there and I couldn't hear them. But I think that made them madder, because no one likes to be ignored. Yet I wasn't going to stop, either.

When I reached the bottom of the stairs, they weren't yelling anymore, so I figured they had lost interest. Up ahead, I could see my father's black Oldsmobile about thirty yards away. *If I can just make it there*, I thought. *And if the car door is unlocked . . . and if it really is his car.*

I tried to speed up a little, while at the same time still looking as if I was walking calmly.

What I really wanted to do was say, "Sorry, I didn't mean to stare at you. And I don't think you look like monkeys." But maybe that would have made them really want to beat me up.

If I could just turn around, I thought, *and see what they're doing. Maybe they were sliding down the rail again and forgotten all about me.* Or maybe they were sneaking up on me, too quiet to hear.

And that was when the first rock hit me, right between my shoulder blades. It sickened me, like when you get the wind knocked out of you and want to throw up. But I didn't know that could happen from behind.

I kept walking, even though I couldn't catch my breath, the pain thudding dull at first, and then expanding in currents through my back and neck, making tears shoot out the corners of my eyes even though I tried to fight them back. If they saw me crying, they would know they had hurt me. And I wanted them to think I didn't even feel the rock.

I kept on walking, and a bunch of other rocks flew by, missing me. A couple of them landed on cars in the parking lot. *Now they'll get in trouble*, I thought, *because you aren't allowed to hit cars with rocks.* But no one seemed to be around, which was strange, because there were always lots of people walking by the museum.

I kept on walking, not turning my head back. Another rock hit me, this one behind my knee, making my leg half-collapse. And that's when I realized that you never hear the ones that hit you. Because you can't hear them throwing it, and you don't hear it land.

A few seconds later, another hit me in the lower back, but that didn't hurt so much because of my loose coat and the rolled-up painting stuck in my back pocket. *Where are they getting the rocks from?* I wondered. There was only concrete and bushes around.

The next one hit the back of my head and hurt so much I lost the noon light for a second. And then the crying surged again, but still I wouldn't let it out and tried to be calm, like my mother said.

Everything else seemed strangely quiet. The Negro kids weren't yelling anymore. I could only hear their missing rocks click against the pavement.

Maybe we're cut off from the Carnegie world somehow, I thought, *and in a separate realm that nobody can see or hear. And it will go on forever, unless I reach my father's car, and then I can get back into the world I used to know.*

But they could still be moving closer, inside the quietness, preparing to kick my face into the concrete without anyone seeing, even though there had to be people coming out of the museum doors by now, especially for lunchtime on the other side of noon. Unless the freezing cold was too much for them to eat outside the Carnegie.

I continued to walk calmly, even when I was just a few feet from my father's car, and even after a rock hit the top of my shoulder, where my coat was padded, so I hardly felt it. Another hit my father's windshield, which startled me. But my hand was already on the door handle, brittle cold, which made me wish I had worn my gloves.

I hesitated to pull on it for fear the car would be locked, and then they would be able to go at me right there against the Oldsmobile, with no one seeing. Because Negroes are invisible from the other side.

As I yanked the silver handle, a rock hit my bare knuckles, sending cold fire shooting into my neck and ears. *They have to be pretty close*, I thought, *to pull off a shot like that.* But at least I didn't have to worry anymore about my mother's "calm walking," because I was inside the car and locking all the doors before they could get there. They never guessed the black Oldsmobile would be my father's car.

They came toward me in single file like someone had given them marching orders. Most were wearing jackets too thin for winter weather, and none had hats or gloves. One tall boy had a brown comb sticking out of the side of his hair. And that's when I noticed that other people were suddenly around—walking down the museum stairs and passing by on the sidewalk, as if closing the car door had broken the spell and the worlds were mixing together again.

Only now the Negro boys were back on the outside, six or seven on a string, each one stopping by the car window to look at me, trying to scare me by making faces with eyes that didn't know me.

Some of their hands touched the window, their palms light-colored and smooth, before they passed on like a movie you watch through glass. Their hands were free, but attached to bodies more trapped than mine.

One of them started swearing again. "Who the fuck do you think you are, anyway?" he said, but not as loud because of the people around.

The last two kids actually made monkey faces at me, which confused me, because I thought they didn't want to be seen as monkeys. And monkeys can't say *fuck you* . . .

They never pulled on the door handles, but they did push down on the back of the car. I didn't care, though, because the Oldsmobile weighed two tons. I remembered our car salesman, Ted Fairchild, pink-faced with gray hair and shaky red hands like a Jesuit's, saying to my father, "This car is just like a tank."

One of them kicked at the trunk, but I still didn't turn around.

Then they passed behind, and I couldn't hear them anymore. And that's when I became aware of how much my body ached from the rocks, especially the back of my head. When I touched, my hand felt sticky blood through the hair, and it made me feel sick again.

A moment later, I saw my father making his way toward the car, his legs moving slowly, his body tilted into the cold wind as if he had been walking that way a long time and not making much progress. A scotch-plaid scarf was wrapped around his neck and tucked inside his black wool coat. He walked with his head down under his black businessman's hat, and that's why he didn't see the rock-throwing boys.

He had no idea I was waiting in the car until he was right up next to it. And he didn't seem surprised. But he did stand still for just a second, and that's when I noticed the flower inside his gloved left hand.

As he opened his door, I could see the worry lines in his face about things he would never tell me. And I knew I wouldn't tell him about the Negro kids throwing rocks. I remembered a Sunday dinner with Uncle Stanley, just after the riots started in the Hill District, and my father saying that "the Negroes should be living back in Africa, because it's only a matter of time before they throw rocks at our windows and walk in through our front door."

And Uncle Stanley saying, in his drinking-mean way, "Ah, you're crazy. They're never going to make it all the way out here. They like burning down their own neighborhoods too much."

Shortly after that, my oldest sister brought her friend Ella, who was a Negro, home from nursing college to have dinner with us and spend the night. And although my father ignored Ella the whole evening, I never heard him talk again about sending the Negroes back to Africa.

He sat down slowly and closed the car door. I could smell the cigarette odor coming from his heavy coat that he unbuttoned using only his right hand, because his other hand still held the flower. He sighed as if he was out of breath, the air from his nose and mouth fogging up the front window.

I wondered if he would notice the crack in the windshield from the rock, but he didn't. So I didn't say anything. I also wondered if he was going to say sorry for being late. But he just stared straight ahead with his head tilted down and said nothing.

Eventually, he put the key in the ignition like it was heavy and hard for him to do.

"What's that flower for?" I asked.

"It's a rose for Sister Emmanuel," he said, slightly out of breath.

By the time we got to Mercy Hospital, it was nearly 1 p.m., and I still hadn't eaten. We passed some vending machines on the way up to Sister Emmanuel's room, but my father was so focused on getting there—gripping the single red rose in his hand—I didn't want to ask him to stop.

My father called her "Patsy," which was her real name before going into the convent at age seventeen and becoming Sister Emmanuel. She was the youngest of eight children in my father's family. When she was born in 1921, my father's mother died. My mother told me nothing was the same for him after that. He was twelve years old.

Eight months later, my grandfather married his dead wife's sister—because "he needed someone to take care of his eight children," my mother said. My mother called her "the witch," because her future mother-in-law's sole purpose was to keep the children away from her new husband. From that point forward, my father lost all contact with his father, the "ear, nose, and throat" doctor, who was, my mother said, a very devout man. My father was sent away to boarding school in Baden, the same place where Patsy would later enter the convent and become Sister Emmanuel. My father never lived at home again.

When we entered the hospital room, Sister Emmanuel wasn't in her bed, which surprised my father.

"I'm over here, dear," a faint voice said from a chair in the corner.

Amazingly, Sister Emmanuel was sitting up, even though her body was severely bent after years of weakening bones and not eating. Her feet, in nun's old black shoes, dangled short of the floor like little girl's feet. And she was smiling, as if she enjoyed seeing us look for her in the wrong place.

A few months earlier, Sister Emmanuel had most of her small intestine removed. It had been blocked up since she was born, my mother said. By age forty-seven, her body was so weakened that her skeleton had actually collapsed, until she was only three and a half feet tall and weighed less than seventy pounds.

Her whole life, she never complained, my mother said. Yet the pain was terrible. And that's why my mother thought Sister Emmanuel should be a saint.

Her spine had become so curved that her head permanently faced the ground. When she talked to you, she propped her chin up with her bone-thin hands, pegging her elbows into her knees, which were not much wider than popsicle sticks.

Yet her face was amazingly young looking. Everyone on my father's side had young faces, but Patsy's face was beatific, my mother said. Sister Emmanuel actually looked how an angel might look, if angels really did exist, after bones wearing down inside a stopped-up body, because God wanted to give her that much . . . except for a few dark hairs shooting out of her cheeks in places, and eyebrows black as my father's, like the hair on his head which never turned gray because of "shoe polish," Uncle Stanley said. "We all know your father uses shoe polish."

"Can we get you anything, Patsy?" my father asked.

"No, dear. I'm fine."

He was still holding his hat and standing behind me as I sat on the edge of the bed. He talked about doctors and hospital matters, while all I wanted to do was ask her about the Negro boys throwing rocks. But I couldn't with my father standing there. Sister Emmanuel understood every kind of human being without ever going anywhere, so she had to understand the Negroes, especially since they lived all around Mount Mercy Hospital and the convent, both of which were at the edge of the Hill District. And she knew all about sadness—like the sadness of the Vietnam War I heard her talking about one time, or of a shooting that happened across the street from the convent. Yet she could still see people as better than they really were, and that's why I liked visiting her.

Her straw-thin fingers took my hand, and she looked at me through her pointed gray glasses, calling me by my first and middle names as only my mother did and asking about my art class. But I only wanted to talk about the Negroes and the stones—like Jesus asking us to cast stones against our self first, or the devil saying he could turn stones into bread if Jesus would only ask, because so many people are hungry. But we can't live on bread alone, He said, even though bread would have been fine since I was so hungry . . .

And Sister Emmanuel living on two crackers a day and just a teaspoon of peanut butter, my mother said—miraculous enough to make her a saint, with no small intestine, and taking sips of water like a raven, which she drank from a shot glass my father gave her when she came to Sunday dinner. Aunt Patsy calling it "God's ale" and laughing about it. And strangers coming from West Virginia and Ohio just to see "the nun who lives on two crackers a day"—like a bird, like a miracle.

But Jesus never performed miracles when people wanted him

to, not even stones into bread, except with the water into wine for his mother, and He wasn't very nice about it. And if the Negro kids had thrown chunks of bread, that wouldn't have hurt so much . . . And if you throw your bread out on the water it will come back sandwiches, my mother always said—unless Sister Emmanuel thought it better to be hit by stones, because then other people would have more bread.

"Have you been eating, Patsy?" my father asked.

"Oh, yes," she said.

But we didn't believe her, even though she couldn't lie.

A nurse came in with a vase, and my father fussed around placing the rose in it.

Have you ever seen a miracle? I wanted to ask.

Sister Emmanuel's head dropped, and her eyes stopped looking at me, as if she'd heard my question somehow and was waiting for a voice to give her the answer from the glorious beatific.

"*You* are a miracle, dear boy," she said, raising her head and touching my hands again with her thin fingers.

She adjusted her hands under her chin so she could look at me better, as if I were the only person in the world at that moment, which was how she looked at everyone.

"Come on, son," my father said. "We don't want to tire out Aunt Patsy. We'll see her again next Saturday."

And my father would bring another red rose, because after he did something once, it became a routine.

Sister Emmanuel still stared at me, her blue-gray eyes watery and certain, as if she'd heard words no one had spoken—maybe something about why the Negro boys could hate me even though they didn't know me.

"Let's hurry," my father said once we were outside in the cold wind.

But I knew it wasn't the cold he worried about, but Mercy Hospital being in "a bad section of town" as he called it. Yet it never seemed to bother Sister Emmanuel, who could have told me what to do about the Negro boys, if I only could have asked her.

ᎷᎪᎷᎪ

"How about a sardine sandwich?" my mother asked.

I didn't really like sardines, but it was two-thirty in the afternoon and I still hadn't eaten, so I didn't object. I knew she would put the sardines on toast with mustard because that was the way she liked it. But it was too strong-tasting for me.

She opened the oblong tin over the sink just in case some of the fish oil spilled. Then she drained it by using the top of the tin to block the fish from falling out. I could smell the sardines right away, even though I was sitting across the kitchen.

Setting the oily fish aside, she opened a can of tomato soup, the jelly-like stuff plopping into the saucepan, followed by a can of milk.

"Do you want some Ritz crackers?" she asked.

"OK."

She poured me a glass of milk and stirred the soup, then bent under the sink to toss the sardine and soup cans into the bin. After dropping two slices of bread into the toaster, she turned toward me, resting her back against the counter.

"So how did your museum class go today?"

"We tried copying one of the famous paintings in the gallery."

"Who was it by?"

"I forget."

"You should try and remember the names of the painters."

"I know. Mr. Fornier told us. I just forget."

"So, how did it go?"

"Not very good."

"Not very well," she said, correcting me.

"I only got a little bit done . . . finished, I mean. Because it was hard concentrating with all the people walking back and forth."

"Did you bring it home?"

"No."

Which was almost the truth, since I hadn't painted exactly what Mr. Fornier wanted us to.

The toast popped up, and she quickly placed the hot slices on a plate and put another slice of bread in and turned around to stir the soup again. She took the Ritz crackers from the cupboard and brought them to the table along with my glass of milk. I thought she might say something about the cut on my knuckles where the rock had hit me, but maybe she didn't notice. Though she surprised me by touching my wrist for a moment, like she was trying to tell me something—maybe about always loving me no matter what, like she used to say when I was young. But now it was just her warm hand, which I could still feel resting on my wrist after she took it away and headed back across the kitchen.

She carried my bowl of soup over between her two hands and then returned to the counter. I watched her fingers separate the sardines, taking out the small, spiny bones and placing them on a Scott towel, and then setting the fish pieces on top of my toast. The oil dripped from her fingers as she spread the mustard, her hand waving back and forth with the knife.

She cut the sandwich in half because my mother believed you should never serve a sandwich whole, then rinsed her hands and dried them on the dish towel and brought my sandwich to the table. Meanwhile, I crumbled a bunch of crackers into my soup, turning it so thick it was hardly like soup anymore.

After making half a sardine sandwich for herself, my mother sat across the table from me and kind of stared blankly while she ate. I sensed she wanted to talk about something but was unsure how to do it. So I avoided her eyes and my mustard and sardine sandwich and dropped my head down to eat my soup.

Lorraine passed through the kitchen, which surprised me, since it was Saturday, and she always came on Monday. But the riots had probably messed up her cleaning schedule.

Lorraine sighed as she reached up in the cupboard for the furniture polish, and then she walked slowly in front of me and headed through the swinging door into the dining room. I could smell the spray polish coming through the door, mixed with the strong smell of Lorraine herself, which used to bother me until I taught myself to connect her smell with Mondays. When I asked my mother about it one time, she said, "The poor thing has had a hard life, and she isn't able to bathe and change clothes like we do."

Sometimes, Lorraine's clothes looked familiar, because when we wanted to throw out our old clothes, my mother would say, "Save it and I'll give it to Lorraine." And leftover food would always be kept until Monday to "give to Lorraine." And when our hands were dirty, they were always "as black as Lorraine's."

She wore a hat fashioned out of newspaper when she worked, pointed on top like the Queen of Hearts. And she always talked to herself, which took me a long time to get used to, especially her moaning voice as she got down on her knees to wipe the baseboards, and then the groaning and talking to herself as she slowly raised her creaking body upright.

"I'm afraid of Lorraine," I said to my mother one day when Lorraine was running the vacuum. I was seven. And she said, "Please don't think that way."

Every Monday, Lorraine's sixteen-dollar check waited for her on the front table. But she wouldn't pick it up until five o'clock as she headed out the door to catch her bus with a bundle of food from our refrigerator under her arm. If the weather was really cold, my mother would drive Lorraine up to the bus stop on Washington Road.

A couple times, when Lorraine was sick and couldn't make it out of her house, my mother would drive all the way across Pittsburgh to the Hill District to take her food and medicine. I didn't know how she even knew where Lorraine lived. But I went with her one time and saw Lorraine's house, a dark wooden structure next to lots of sad-looking red-brick apartments. I wondered how she had enough room in the small house for her whole family, especially for her daughter's eight children who also lived there.

My father never liked my mother driving to the Hill District, because he thought it was too dangerous going "where anybody but the Negroes should be afraid to go." But maybe he was just worried about not getting his dinner on time.

"I didn't know Lorraine was here today," I said, looking up from my soup.

"Don't leave your spoon in the bowl. Rest it on the plate when you're not using it."

"But I am using it . . ."

"She needs the money. And I have no idea how she got here, since the buses aren't running down Fifth Avenue."

"How come?"

"Because they've been throwing rocks at the bus windows. So the bus drivers refuse to go into the Hill District."

"How will Lorraine get home, then?"

"I'm going to drive her."

"But what if they throw rocks at you?"

"Lorraine will be in the car with me. I'm not going to tell your father, though. You tell him after I've left."

I imagined my mother in her wavy gray hair driving our old Rambler into the Hill District to Lorraine's house, where there were too many children's names to remember. But my mother knew them all.

"They just keep having babies," my father said one time. "And they can't take care of them. It's a disgrace."

And I wasn't sure if he was talking about Lorraine's family or about all of the Negroes in Pittsburgh, or about all Negroes everywhere.

"I can go with you," I said.

"No, you just got back. And your father has something waiting for you . . . downstairs."

"What do you mean?"

"You have to go see. It's a surprise. As soon as you finish your lunch, go on down. I think he's in the garden room, or the garage."

But I kept thinking about Lorraine's family, and how much I wanted to meet them, even though I never thought about them that much before. I especially wanted to meet the granddaughter named "Toomey," because Lorraine's daughter thought she had a tumor growing inside her and didn't know it was a baby. Afterwards, the daughter ran away, and Lorraine had to take care of Toomey and all her brothers and sisters. And that's when my mother started giving Lorraine extra money my father didn't know about. "Cash in hand," my mother called it, separate from the weekly check.

I could hear Lorraine talking to herself in the dining room. And I could see her, even though the swinging door was closed—her large, stooped figure bending over and sighing, talking out loud as if she were two people, while she polished the dark mahogany furniture.

Soon she'll make her way to the dining room window, I thought, where the Creelys saw her one time from the front yard just as dusk was coming on—Lorraine standing before the lighted window, reaching up high to clean the top panes of glass, her arms moving back and forth rhythmically, and Frank Creely saying, "Your cleaning lady looks like a gorilla."

So I asked my mother why we had a black cleaning lady when everyone else in the neighborhood seemed to have white ones, and their cleaning ladies babysat sometimes and were more like grandmas you could get to know, but Lorraine would never be like that with me because she barely looked at me on Mondays and never

146

talked, except to herself. And my mother said I shouldn't worry so much about other people, and that's when I told her about the Creelys saying Lorraine looked like a gorilla. And even though my mother couldn't stand yelling, she raised her voice to me: "Never say that about Lorraine again! Do you hear?"

And I never did. But my mind would think it sometimes, even though I told myself not to, as if the Creelys had gotten inside me and wouldn't go away, which is why I felt guilty whenever I saw Lorraine at the dining room window—because I would think "gorilla" before I could catch myself. Because there really are two people inside us—one always disappointing the other, even more than our mothers would be disappointed if they knew what we were thinking, which is why it really was OK for Lorraine to talk to herself.

"Is there something the matter with your sandwich?" my mother asked.

"No . . . Why?"

"You're not eating it."

"I will."

But I couldn't even look at it. That's what happens when you wait too long—your hunger turns the food strange, until a sardine sandwich seems like something that shouldn't be eaten. So I finished my soup instead, and drank my milk. Because the less you have to chew on, the less strange the food seems.

Lorraine passed into the kitchen again to get a duster out of the closet. I wanted to say something to her, but didn't know how.

She went back through the swinging door, and my mother brought up the sardines again.

"Let the sandwich go. I can wrap it up for Lorraine. Go downstairs and see what's there. And find your father."

So I did, even though I really wanted to stay upstairs and talk with Lorraine. Because she had been with our family so long, and I wanted to know what it was like being a Negro.

Downstairs, in the middle of the wood-paneled room, was a pool table right where the ping-pong table used to be. Under the fluorescent lights, everything seemed unreal, as if I had walked into someone else's basement by not paying attention when I passed between floors.

I looked for my father. But he wasn't in the garden room or the furnace room or the laundry room or out in the garage. So I went back upstairs, where my mother was busy wrapping up my sandwich in a brown paper bag.

"How did he do that?"

"I don't know. It was delivered this morning when you were at the museum. He always says he doesn't know where he'll get the eight hundred dollars every month I need to run the house. But then he always does . . . Just let him know how surprised you are."

"But if we don't have any money, I don't want it."

I went back to the basement and found my father in the garden room, bending over his flats of dahlia bulbs. Maybe he had been there all along and I had missed him somehow. Even though it was winter, he had his summer garden clothes on, including his blue soft sneakers, which wouldn't keep his thin toes warm.

"I can't believe there's a pool table here," I said, trying to sound excited.

He continued to spread peat moss over his dahlia bulbs and didn't say anything. But his eyes looked at me over the rims of his glasses.

"Where did you get it?" I asked.

"I made a deal," he said. "With a client."

"Do you want to play a game?" I asked.

"Not now, son. You go ahead. I'll play with you some other time."

But I could see in his face that we would never play another time. And I knew I would never ask again.

He stepped into the garage and left the door open, and the cold February air rushed in. I walked over to close it and heard him call from the back of the garage, "Wait, son. I'm coming right back."

ᐱᔓᐱᔓᐱ

I forgot to put the lamp on before lying down. But it was OK, because I was enjoying the gray-dark coming on, passing through the attic windows of my third-floor bedroom, mixing into the older darkness that was already there.

Without a lamp on, you can watch the window light disappear until it doesn't matter anymore.

The mattress springs kept creaking every time I made the slightest move. My sister said it's the price you pay for moving to the third floor—I'd have to sleep on a hard bed with old springs underneath that made it difficult even to think steady. And everyone below hears you through the ceiling, like I used to hear my brother creaking the springs at night when he was up on the third floor.

I thought about going back to the basement and trying out the pool table after all. But I'd have to walk past my father, pacing back and forth in the living room, and I didn't want to face seeing him. I wished the pool table wasn't there, and that I didn't have to worry about it. But the guilt makes you think about it anyway—three floors down, under the thick concrete ceiling that Mr. Morian, our furnace man, said an atomic bomb couldn't destroy, making our basement "an ideal fallout shelter," with the darkness always arriving there ahead of time, and the dampness, too, which is why my mother bought a dehumidifier my father always turned off because "it wastes electricity."

I tried not to think about my mother driving to the Hill District, where the boys sit on front stoops in the cold, keeping watch on their street, and where the city buses are afraid to go because the rocks can fall like hail from Negro hands . . . unless they see Lorraine first, then there wouldn't be any rocks, because they're more used to seeing themselves in the dark than we are. So they will notice her sitting quietly next to my mother who talks on and on, Lorraine occasionally nodding, her gray Negro hair covered in a purple babushka, saying, "Yes, Mrs. . . . Yes."

"Where's your mother?" my father yelled upstairs to me.

I didn't know he was on the second floor.

"She went to drive Lorraine home."

"To the Hill District?"

And I should be in the car with her, I wanted to say, because I could keep watch for the boys from the museum and see the rocks in their hands before my mother could. But she was already driving through the Hill and I couldn't get to her. And she could leave the earth unseen, with Lorraine by her side . . .

"Did you know it was snowing?" my father asked, opening the door at the bottom of the stairs so I could hear him better. "Your mother hates driving in the snow," he added.

"I didn't know . . . Don't worry. She'll be back in time to fix dinner."

My father wouldn't come up the stairs, because he never came to the third floor—which made me wonder if he'd ever ascended to the third floor in his family home when he was a boy, living on Vernon Drive in a house I had seen one time . . . a large white house with a green tile roof and large windows in front and porches on either side. But his third floor wasn't attic-like, so maybe it wasn't the same when he was looking for a place to escape to, on a late afternoon in summer, maybe, when he was thirteen, just before he would be sent away to Baden.

. . . up the staircase that opens into white air, his hand holding

the rounded top of the banister as he makes the turn and then pauses on the landing to stare out the large picture window facing the street, but not long enough to sit on the casement; and then moving slowly because of not knowing where; touching his forehead with his hand, unaware of his own gesture but still keeping watch on himself from the outside; wondering near the top just how much time he needs before he can feel better, with nowhere to go for that to happen, because he sees the white air but not a way through it; so he listens to the minutes and thinks of his father making his buggy rounds led by a horse named Rosy; because he wants to tell his father something that his father will never hear, after arriving home at 7pm because his dead wife's sister-wife served dinner like German clockwork at 7pm, my mother said, on the summer porch across a long table with unsteady legs, so you couldn't put too much weight on it, except for his father, whose arms are so thin; the table with more than enough room for eight children who can see their father but not talk to him because she won't let them, with his gentle head bent over his food because of stooped shoulders, "a family trait," my mother said . . .

Behind glasses, his forehead skin so thin you can see the texture of bone; and a weak man, my mother always said, because he never interfered with his wife's sister-wife keeping the children away; even though Aunt Patsy said if you imagine a saint looking down at you, that is your grandfather, with God's kindness so you don't have to wonder anymore when you pray about what kindness looks like . . . little sister Patsy in her wooden high-chair always sitting next to him, not knowing that her father's love for her was different, and her brothers and sisters not noticing it at first either, because they were more interested in getting enough to eat, which was never a money problem but only a German problem, my mother said; because Patsy's stepmother decided how much food should be enough, and there was never more; which is why no one at the table noticed little sister Patsy hardly eating anything, on the quiet porch inside the failing light with the thin white curtains blowing inward and touching their father's shoulders, and the muffled voices from other children playing on Vernon Drive coming through the screened windows while the doctor's children were still eating, missing that perfect playtime—the space between almost-dark and when the streetlights come on, when twilight really does exist for a while . . .

But my father's dinner progressed so slowly, as if time was barely moving on the fading porch, during the slow masticating of the food and even the milk, because his father believed that the body was incapable of absorbing anything quickly, but which my mother blamed on the Germans, not the Irish, with my father's great, great Irish grandfather being the most famous harpist in all of Northern Ireland, she said, living to be one hundred and twelve while hardly eating anything, like Sister Emmanuel, and carried around on a cot during his last years while still performing even though he was blind and had a huge wen on his head . . .

And then someone from the electric company decides twilight is over and turns the street lights on, because someone somewhere always decides things like that; making all the parents on Vernon Drive say in the next second: "It's getting dark. Time to come home." Because we're never patient enough and miss the evening's moments passing around us, that my father always loved, even from his porch chair, wanting to talk to his father . . .

I had moved to the third floor when my older brother went away to medical school, just like he had done when my oldest brother went away to college, a brother I didn't really know until I was four years old and he came home from Holy Cross, bringing the girl he was going to marry. It was late at night, but I spied on her from the top of the stairs with my sister, both of us kneeling on the landing as she walked in the door and stood uncomfortably next to the lamp by the front table. It was the first time a woman looked beautiful to me, so I loved her, and told my sister. The next day at breakfast, my sister told the whole family, and I thought I would never forgive her.

And that's why you need a third floor attic to go to . . . the third floor becoming the "final purpose" you learn about in school when Father Larkin explains the Greek word "telos"—a goal that makes your life worthwhile.

But my ascent was too late. The third-floor bedroom would always be my brothers' place no matter how hard I tried to take it over. So, after a while, I put their stuff back in the dresser and desk and took my things downstairs—a Clemente baseball card and some old coins, my first Communion missal, a scapular, a rusty Cub Scout knife, a copy of *White Fang*, and some stupid stones I had taken from the creek one time that didn't seem to mean anything anymore. And the slingshot I never showed Taddy Keegan . . . because what Father Larkin said wasn't true. There is no *telos*.

I lay down on the bed, my head still aching from where the stone had hit it. I remembered the dried blood and thought about getting up to wash it off, but I didn't move, trying all the while to forget about the pool table in the basement that I didn't deserve, coming from my father's no-money.

I was barely breathing in the darkness, so the bed wouldn't creak and I could listen for the closing of the front door, two floors away, and my mother coming home. Through the walls and ceilings, I could see my father pacing across the darkened living room, waiting for her, too, and wondering about his dinner, his second bourbon highball finished and a third one not yet allowed.

Every now and then, he would peek out the window at the snow, wishing he could hear it, like rain. Because rain is something you can disappear into, until even the creaking sounds don't matter anymore,

Beyond the third-floor windows, I thought I could actually hear the snowflakes, unless it was just the wind blowing against the panes, my eyes taking forever to adjust to the vague light that really isn't there until you imagine seeing it, but different from Dulaney's Cave where the vague light never arrives.

I could smell the oils from my painting just across the room, and almost see the canvas half curled on my brothers' dresser, the white edges fading into purplish black.

I will have to tell Noni, I thought, *just to see what she says about how I painted myself into the famous gallery work we were supposed to copy, of the women gathering water in large urns by the stream. Barely twelve hours ago . . .* Mr. Fornier never looked that closely at my painting, so he missed seeing the Pittsburgh boy lying asleep against the hill, inside the old Dutch canvas.

My mother will come in the front door and he will say—"Where have you been?" Like he always does. As if she had been someplace exciting, rather than driving through the Hill District in the snow . . . with Lorraine probably recognizing some of the boys on the street while my mother talks on, trying to get rid of her nerves. Not driving fast, because in her whole life my mother never drove fast, especially in the snow, which was falling on the Hill District and on Seminole Drive, and all over the Pittsburgh in-between . . . that my father misses because of his pacing, except when he stops at the living room window to see the flakes that seem almost stuck in the air, making me want to get up and look, too—at the snow you can't hear even with the light on outside, while still waiting to put the lamp on inside, to see if the boy in the painting really is there. Because who can see a painting in the dark anyway?

The Rivers

I didn't hear about it until everyone was ready to head downtown. Craig McCann stopped by in a hurry, his body wiggling and his hand jabbing at his thick glasses as he stood on our front steps.

He talked sideways at me. "You don't want to miss this," he said excitedly. "The Keegans are taking their two-man raft down to the rivers. Taddy says he's going to jump off the 'Bridge to Nowhere.'"

Then Craig McCann ran up the street as if he were heading to an emergency and cut through old man Hoover's yard and disappeared. A few minutes later, I was cutting through my own backyard. The June day was hot and cloudless, and the white, humid sky seemed to press upon me as I made my way to Taddy Keegan's house.

His older brother's cab was parked in front—a "hack," Paddy Keegan called it. And Taddy and his younger brother Timmy were stuffing a deflated yellow raft and two plastic oars into the trunk. Paddy, who was in his twenties and one of the curly-haired Keegans, yelled in a controlled way that Taddy and Timmy seemed used to: "Hurry up, you little shits. And remember, I'm just going to drop you off downtown. You have to find your own way home."

"We can take the trolley," Timmy said defiantly. "I have the thirty-five cents."

No one said anything to me. And I wasn't sure if it was because they didn't want me there or because they were too focused on getting down to the rivers.

Taddy sat up front and, without even asking, I sat down in the back next to Timmy. A second later, Paddy made the car explode away from the curb so suddenly our heads jerked back.

"Hey! There's McCann!" I said.

We could see him running down the cobbled bricks of Nakoma and waving at Paddy to stop, which he did, slamming on the brakes so hard that the back tires screeched and slapped up against the curb. Since Paddy didn't own the cab, he didn't seem to care what happened to it.

"Hurry up, McCann!" Paddy yelled through Taddy's open window.

McCann climbed nervously into the backseat right on top of Timmy's legs because Timmy wouldn't move over. Then they started pushing at each other, and the car took off with the door still open and McCann not all the way in.

Paddy drove downtown in a way that only a cab driver would know, climbing up the steep back streets of Beechview, the car feeling hotter and hotter even with the windows open, then bumping across the bricks and trolley tracks that swerved the cab like an amusement park ride. All the while, I kept thinking how much easier it would be just to take Liberty Avenue straight downtown.

"How you gonna blow this thing up?" Paddy yelled in a bothered voice. "Because I'm just gonna drop you off on the South Side. That's it."

"How about stopping at a gas station?" Taddy asked.

Surprisingly, Paddy did, at the bottom of Mount Washington. But the blown-up raft didn't fit back inside the trunk. So Paddy said they'd have to hold it up on the roof by gripping the edges, which

Taddy did from one side of the car and Timmy from the other.

"We're not going through the Liberty Tunnel," Paddy said, "because it's probably illegal with a raft on the roof. So we'll take the McArdle Roadway and go over Mount Washington. I'll drive slow so you guys can hold on."

But we only got a little ways up the hill before Timmy's fingers couldn't hold the rubber edge any longer and the raft blew off the roof and bounced back down the road and into the cars behind us. Paddy pulled over, but before getting out, he turned around and smacked Timmy's forehead several times with the palm of his hand, calling him a "useless idiot."

"Ah, me Irish matey," Timmy said, as if he didn't really mind his older brother slapping his face, "do ya hafta be so cruel?"

"C'mon, Paddy," Taddy said. "Quit giving Timmy the business and let's go get the raft."

So the two of them ran off behind the car, and Timmy continued talking fake Irish with his eyes closed as if he was in a trance.

After putting the raft back on the roof, Taddy offered to drive so Paddy could try holding on.

"You assholes ain't insured to drive my hack," Paddy said.

Which surprised me, because he didn't say anything about we assholes being only fourteen.

So Paddy held the raft with one hand and steered with the other, and Taddy held onto the other side. And Timmy kept mumbling Irish as the cab inched its way up to Mount Washington, and then down the steep other side, with all of Pittsburgh suddenly coming into view and the steel mills steaming in the distance, and the cars tooting us from behind until we finally stopped next to the old Pittsburgh rail station alongside the Monongahela River. The station had been closed for years, the glass roof still blackened from World War II when they painted it that way, my father said, so the German planes wouldn't see it when they came to bomb Pittsburgh. Because

Pittsburgh was the industrial capital of the country, my father said. "It turned out more tons of steel than any city in the world,"

McCann and I sat on the concrete wall and stared across the river at all the businesspeople at Point Park enjoying their lunch outside. *This is the kind of thing you do*, I thought, *when you're older and out of school—just sit around on a hot day and watch the river and stare at the city and everything else that exists beyond.*

"You guys are on your own now," Paddy said, looking back as he got inside his cab.

Through the open window, he added, "And be careful, you little shits. Don't get into any trouble."

The car spit gravel as it took off, and in that second I realized Paddy had no idea what his brother Taddy was planning to do. He probably thought Taddy and Timmy were just going to float around in the rivers and enjoy their raft, and McCann and I would just loaf around and watch them.

When Taddy and Timmy finally got into the raft, they started arguing about who was in front and who was in back, until it seemed they might turn the raft over into the filthy Monongahela. And that would be the end of it.

But they quieted, and Taddy let Timmy's end be the front. Paddling together, they headed across the wide brown river toward the Point.

"What are we gonna do now?" McCann asked.

"I don't know."

"We should go to the other side where we can watch them better."

"How are we going to get there?"

"Across the Fort Pitt Bridge."

"But there's no walking allowed on Fort Pitt Bridge."

"That's why we have to run real fast," McCann said.

So we streaked across the bridge where there wasn't even a

sidewalk, but only a concrete curb between the cars racing by and the railing. Smelling the thick river inside the waves of heat, I never looked up or down, but only at McCann's sneakers flashing back at me in quick rhythm.

When we reached the end, we ran towards the Hilton Hotel, and then through the pedestrian tunnel underneath the Fort Pitt Monument, and finally up the other side and onto the lawn at Point Park. Sweating and thirsty, we didn't stop until we reached the edge of the Allegheny River near the Bridge to Nowhere.

Taddy and Timmy were still out in the middle of the water where the three rivers merged together. They didn't seem to be getting anywhere with their paddling. They'd stop for a bit, as if they were giving up. Then they'd paddle again without making progress. Occasionally, motorboats zoomed by as if they didn't see Taddy and Timmy. But I could see them.

After a while, they decided they couldn't make it to the bridge against the current and turned horizontal and rowed to shore right near where McCann and I were standing.

"At least you made it into the Allegheny River," I said as Taddy climbed out.

He didn't look at me or say a word, but just started walking robot-like along the concrete river wall toward the Bridge to Nowhere.

Timmy didn't say anything either, which was unusual. I couldn't tell if he was mad at his brother or just mad at the river. He started dragging the raft along the shore in a drudging way, trying to follow close behind Taddy. Eventually, Timmy re-entered the water and floated out toward the middle, where the Bridge to Nowhere ended in midair.

While I was watching him, I lost track of Taddy Keegan. I couldn't spot him anywhere. *Maybe he's already climbing the bridge*, I thought. And that's when I remembered him talking one time about driving off the end of the Bridge to Nowhere, just like some crazy college kid did a few years before—in an old Chrysler station wagon, right through the barriers at full speed, miraculously landing unhurt on the far shore of the Allegheny River. He did it on a dare, Taddy said, because that's how things get done. So Taddy Keegan thought he could do it, too, if only someone would let him drive his car.

The whole incident upset my father. "It's an embarrassment," he said to Uncle Stanley, "for a city with more bridges than any city in the country to have one ending in midair."

After the main span was completed, there were problems with the property owners on the other side, my father said, which was too bad because the bridge was supposed to lead to a new football stadium so the Steelers wouldn't have to play in "lousy old Pitt Field anymore," which was up past the Hill District where my father hated to go. But the new stadium hadn't been built either.

Taddy Keegan had climbed the bridge after all. I could see him moving steady along the upper level of the roadway. But the noon-time crowds hadn't noticed him yet. There were so many other things for them to look at. Who was going to see a boy balanced against the handrail, with his feet near where the green barrels were arranged at the end of the Bridge to Nowhere?

Fifty yards below, Timmy floated almost perfectly still in his small yellow raft. I looked for McCann, but he had run up toward the bridge. I decided to stay, though, because Timmy was yelling to his brother. People on the Point heard him, his voice taking them right out of their unslanted sunlight:

"Brudder! Brudder!" Timmy yelled. "Don't jump! Don't jump!"

His words sounded familiar because I had heard him talk like that before, once when I came across him and Taddy down at the creek just as it was getting dark. I heard them before I could see them, because the dusk light was mixing it up with the evening mist. So I followed the sound of their voices across the damp grass until I was right next to the creek. They were standing inside the opening of the sewer tunnel that passed underneath the Iroquois dead end.

"Brudder, brudder," Timmy said, "how could you make a lad do such a thing?"

"Then pay me what you owe me," Taddy said.

"I don't got it, brudder. But I'm good for it. I'm good for it, brudder."

"Then you have to blow me," Taddy said.

They both saw me standing there at the same moment but didn't seem to care, and continued on as if they were performing in a play and I was the only audience. And I wasn't really there either.

Their words sounded serious, but their acting was kind of funny, maybe because I could hardly see them through the dimming gray light.

"But brudder," Timmy said, "how do I know ye won't piss in me mouth? Oh, brudder, brudder, ye know I'm good for the money."

I'd heard about blowing, because everyone used the word. I just wasn't really sure how it happened. But I knew it was wrong, especially between brothers.

"OK. I'll do it, but without touching ye, brudder," Timmy said.

The sound of the creek was louder than usual. Then a truck passed by up on Gilkeson Road and drowned out even the creek water.

When Taddy unzipped his pants, I thought about leaving. But I wanted to know what they did.

I looked up toward Gilkeson Road and thought how it was a good thing Little Kenny wasn't here. And when I looked back, Timmy was bending over inside the tunnel darkness getting ready to put his mouth around it without touching, because then it would be a sin. I heard his breath blow twice, before he suddenly stood up and stepped outside the tunnel onto a creek rock.

"Now we're even-Stevens, brudder. Right? Even-Stevens?"

Taddy didn't say anything, but turned and headed inside the

tunnel, where it was too dark to see him. But I could hear his feet splashing through the water, the sound gradually fading until it was lost inside the rolling creek water.

Timmy stepped onto the grass and walked past me as if he didn't see me, as if I were behind a one-way glass, and he headed towards Kaufman's Hill and his home beyond . . .

When Taddy didn't answer, Timmy repeated, "Brudder! Brudder! Don't jump!"

"I'm gonna jump! I'm gonna jump!" Taddy finally yelled back.

He was standing on top of the bridge railing, leaning against the last suspension pole, his hair sticking straight up from sweat and his arms raised as if he were signaling triumph. Some of the Point people cupped their hands over their eyes to see him better through the noon sunlight.

Timmy somehow stood up in the little raft and yelled the same thing again, and Taddy yelled back in the same way. And it went on like that for a while, until everyone on the Point was focused on the two kids and their Irish acting that may have seemed real to some of them. But I knew the difference, because I had heard Timmy talk like that at other times—in our backyard with my father one time. It was a warm night and my father was listening to the ballgame on his little transistor radio that sat in its leather case on the garden wall. Through my third-floor window, I could hear the hurried baseball announcer's voice, but not his words . . . and then Timmy Keegan's crazy Irish yelling.

I went down to the second floor and then halfway down to the first floor, stopping on the landing. Through the window, I could see Timmy Keegan standing on the flagstones in the lower backyard. And instead of pacing around smoking cigarettes and listening to the game, my father was answering back in the same crazy Irish, like he knew it somehow. I could see them fairly well through the screen even though it was already dark outside. And it was strange, because

Timmy never visited my house. Maybe he was just cutting through our yard and ran into my father.

The exchange ended quickly when my mother opened the back door and told them to quiet down because they were scaring the neighbors, even though she didn't really like the crabby old Macbeths who lived next door.

Timmy ran through the poplar trees in our upper backyard and my father came inside, where my mother sat at the gray kitchen table paying the bills.

"Mother, stop being at me," he said loudly.

She jumped up to close the window even though it was a warm night, because she hated yelling and didn't want the neighbors to hear.

My father headed into the dining room to pace there instead, in the almost darkness because no one had put the lamp on yet, and missing the ballgame still playing on his transistor radio outside. He smoked in circles around the dark mahogany table that had been polished by Lorraine until it shined, so you could see, even in the dim light, my father's image inside the dark wood and then back out of it . . . circling around, rubbing his fingers nervously against his palms, his slicked back hair shiny in the window light, and the gray cigarette smoke rising silvery and circling with a motion all its own in the twilight room before fading into the dark corners . . . my father's head down the whole time except when he looked up for a second as he made the turn to pace back the other way.

Still floating under the Bridge to Nowhere, Timmy Keegan yelled again, "Brudder! Brudder! Don't jump!"

But Taddy Keegan was already gone. And I was almost too late to see, except for the last dark shape of him against the brightness, his arms still above his head through the downfall sunlight into the Allegheny River that looked black and distant under the noon sky.

He stayed underwater for a long time—so long that most of

the people at the Point began to believe he wasn't coming up again. And I started counting the seconds to see how long he could last. I thought of yelling out to Timmy, who was peering over the raft into the dark water. He would give the raft a little spin, then look some more. And I wondered why he didn't just jump in and try to save his brother—unless maybe this was part of their act, too.

I considered swimming out myself into the steel mill-polluted water, because Taddy had saved me from drowning in the creek when we rode truck tires after a storm. He pulled me by my hair until I was free of the current.

So I started running up-river, kicking off my shoes along the way so I was ready to jump in, and trying to remember my junior safety lessons so I would be able to save Taddy Keegan if I found him. And that's when he shot up out of the water without his shirt on, like a white-bodied fish, right next to the raft.

All the people at the Point clapped as Taddy climbed in, as if it were the end of a stage show, and he and Timmy started screaming, "Brudder! Brudder!" They hugged each other, kissed on both cheeks, and hugged again. And the Point people clapped again.

Typical Keegan crap, I thought. And it went on until the Point people started losing interest. Because in their minds, the boys were safe now, so there was nothing else to worry about. Meanwhile, the boys were already floating away on the currents of the Allegheny, heading toward the Ohio River.

I had no idea what to do. The sun seemed to get hotter every second and there weren't any ripples of wind on the river, but the currents were still there, taking Taddy Keegan away no matter what, he and Timmy drifting without using the oars. I watched them as they made a little turn and entered the Ohio River, and then they disappeared behind some buildings.

They'll keep drifting west, I thought, *until they come to Neville Island, where they'll get out and try to take a bus home. But they'll have to leave the raft behind, which Taddy won't want to do. So they'll just keep on drifting, right past Neville Island . . .*

I wanted to yell, "Taddy! Taddy!" And I didn't know why. But it was too late for that.

Most of the businesspeople were heading back to work. And the ones left behind seemed to have already forgotten about the boy who jumped off the Bridge to Nowhere.

I stayed longer, sitting on the river wall, trying to fool myself into not worrying about how I was going to get home. Craig Mc-Cann had already left for his father's office downtown. But I didn't want to go to my father's office in the Frick Building and see him pacing around the piles of papers and folders, stopping for a moment to say, "Hi, son," without any surprise in his voice or face, and then continuing his pacing. And I couldn't call my mother, because she didn't even know where I was.

So I would have to take the trolley home alone, even though I had never done that before. And I only had a quarter.

I found myself walking across Point Park as if I wasn't in charge of my own body—back through the pedestrian tunnel and Hilton Plaza to a trolley stop on Liberty Avenue.

42/38 Mt. Lebanon/Beechview, I remembered, was the streetcar I needed to take. And I kept thinking it was too bad Taddy Keegan wasn't there. Because he would find an Irish way to get us on the red trolley car, and we'd look out the window together at all the things that existed beyond.

Some sparrows were making a racket underneath the roof of the trolley stop, bothering me so much I looked around for a stone to throw at them. And that's how I found an old nickel on the pavement by the curb. *I only need another nickel now*, I thought.

The birds kept up their noise, flying in and out of their nest up in the rafter like it was an exciting thing to do. I thought about throwing the nickel at them, but instead walked around with my head down looking for another nickel.

Maybe I should just sneak onto the trolley, I thought. *Because that's what Taddy Keegan would do. But if I can just find a nickel . . .*

I tried using my eyes without dropping my head, so no one would know what I was doing. And I kept thinking—the trolley could be here any minute. *But maybe the nickel won't matter that much to the conductor man*, I thought. *And he will let me take the 42/38 for just thirty cents. And then I will make it home.*

The Lake

When we went up to Lake Erie in August, my sister said it would probably be for the last time. And I wondered how she could be so sure.

"The water is too polluted," she said. "Nobody wants to swim in it anymore."

We were driving in our old black Oldsmobile, sitting on blankets and beach towels so there was more room in the trunk for other stuff. The windows were open because it was hot, and my father's cigarette ash kept blowing back in on me, which is why my sister always sat on the other side.

My mother sometimes asked my father to use the ashtray. But it was useless trying to get him to change anything. He liked using the window, and I would just have to get used to being stung occasionally on my arms and cheek from the cigarette sparks.

"Maybe we can take an ocean vacation next year," my mother said. "The children have never seen the ocean."

"There might not be a vacation next year," my father said, his head hanging low, his eyes looking through the steering wheel more than over it.

Even the Creelys were taking an ocean vacation, and they made fun of me for still going to "dirty ol' Lake Erie, where there aren't even any big waves." Not like Stone Harbor in New Jersey, where they went. But I didn't care, because who'd want to vacation with Creelys anyway?

A few hours later, we arrived at dusk at Madison-on-the-Lake, turning left at the old Lake Store and heading down our street, the grayish lake suddenly appearing, as it always did, unreal in the near-distance—a giant pool widening with our approach and almost blending in with the gray-white sky.

The car stopped on a bed of pine needles in front of Green Gables, the house we rented every year. Vicki, our old Kerry Blue terrier, scratched my legs with her nails as she scrambled to get out of the car first. After taking some of the suitcases in, my father announced he was going to take a late evening dip, leaving my mother and sister and me to unpack the rest of the car.

"It's too dark to swim," my mother said. "You won't be able to see."

"I don't need to see to swim," he said.

My brother was supposed to catch a ride from medical school and meet us at the lake, but he wasn't at the cottage when we arrived. I figured he was already over at his old girlfriend's house, because my brother owned Lake Erie in August. Gail Pagalis's father even let my brother drive his Greek wooden speedboat whenever my brother wanted. Sometimes, my brother and Gail would stop the speedboat in front of our beach, and I'd swim out, trying not to touch my feet on the rocks and seaweed, and climb in. And he would drive fast across the waves to try and scare me, the speedometer reaching almost fifty, the boat smelling like gasoline and the wooden bottom looking as if it could splinter into a million pieces with each crash down between the waves. My brother didn't care, though, because Gail Pagalis was standing close to him. He'd roll his head back and holler into the motorboat wind, "I ain't cool! I ain't cool!"

I had to use the bathroom, so I walked through the house toward the backyard, because the only bathroom was off the back porch. The house floors were covered with a layer of sand even though we had just arrived, which meant my mother would get out the broom. And the whole place smelled cloudy and damp.

The bathroom door didn't close tight because it was warped. So I looked behind me while standing at the toilet to see if anyone was peeking through the crack. But I never knew if anyone was.

When I went back outside, my father was already in his bathing suit and brown terrycloth beach jacket, heading for the steep wooden stairs down to the beach. I had never seen my father change clothes so quickly. Maybe he really was worried about the dark.

A moment later, he faded from my view, and I could only hear the padding of his feet on the sandy steps. I followed partway down, then stopped. Everything was quiet, except for the sound of the waves dragging back against the shore rocks.

I couldn't see my father because of the bushes at the bottom of the stairs, but I knew he was sitting on the last step putting his skinny feet into his old lake sneakers, his last act of preparation before making his way across the beach to the water. I wondered if he really enjoyed going in so late, or if he just did it because he had always done it. Either way, you couldn't question his late evening dip any more than you could question the Lake Erie sunset.

In the morning, it would be the same thing again, getting up for his "early morning dip" just because he had done it once. Which is why my father hated doing anything new, because it could turn into another routine he'd be stuck with forever.

I could see the vague shape of him moving beyond the bushes, but I still didn't want to go down. He was walking slowly and unevenly across the twilight beach, his thin legs posting like sticks under his belly and his head down to see where to step next as he entered the lake water. The low, breaking waves frothed white in the darkness, and his arms were outstretched for balance as he tried not to slip on the mossy round rocks under his feet.

But he never stopped his progress through the graying water—not like when I would go in and freeze knee-deep, fighting the certain truth that I either had to dive quickly or suffer slowly, all the while wishing to be delivered somehow, maybe swept up into the sky or behind closed eyes wake up in my own bed again . . . until the courage came back and I didn't care anymore about the cold black water or landing belly first into the rocks below, which would scratch my chest because I didn't go out far enough, causing me to jerk crazily into deeper water, my eyes closed and arms moving hard against the flat lake, trying not to smell . . .

My father was almost waist deep when he dove in and began his slow crawl into the closing darkness of lake and sky. I couldn't see him, but I could hear his soft splashing and see silver shimmerings across the waves reflected from mysterious light somewhere. Then, a few moments later, his voice above the lake water: "Ahhwooooooah!" bubbling high-pitched out of the darkness. "Ahhwooooooah!"—the only silly sound my father ever made, letting the entire lake world know he was there.

Aunt Frankie arrived the next morning, passing by me in her yellow Mustang as I walked to the Lake Store to get my father's newspapers. When I got back to Green Gables, she was sitting at the breakfast table smoking cigarettes and telling a story that made my mother and sister laugh.

After breakfast, everyone headed down to the beach, including Aunt Frankie, who sat in her sand chair with a cigarette hanging from her lips, applying lotion to her arms. She had the whitest skin of any woman in Pittsburgh, my father said. Uncle Ted, her husband, always told her to keep out of the sun because he didn't believe a woman should get tanned. But Uncle Ted never came to Lake Erie, so Aunt Frankie sat in the sun all day, her orange hair piled high in a spiral so that, when she talked, it wagged just a bit, especially when she gestured with her cigarette hand, the red lipstick mark on the white filter almost hypnotizing until I couldn't think of anything else.

They chatted about things that didn't interest me. My sister, reading in her beach chair, wasn't paying attention. And neither was my father, who sat next to the tree stump where he served drinks at six o'clock.

I cleared some rocks and lay down on my stomach to sleep. But my eyes stayed open, watching Aunt Frankie's freckled hand stab a white cigarette butt into a mound of gray sand.

When I would start to drift off, I'd hear her loud laugh again and watch her hand moving in circles with the lipstick-ringed cigarette. Eventually, the rings became fainter, but then she'd apply more bright red lipstick and the rings were solid again.

Around noon, my brother showed up and wanted to throw the football around. Which I did, even though I hated running on the beach because of the dead fish lying around and the partially hidden rocks that could stub your toes.

He lost interest after a while, and ran into the water and I went back to lie down on my towel. Two more red-lipped cigarettes were in the mound of sand, like little soldiers kissed before death. I watched her hand move again from knee to mouth, and back to her white knee, until I gradually fell asleep.

The next thing I knew, my mother was standing up, announcing that she was heading to the cottage to make lunch. She walked toward the stairs, and I watched Aunt Frankie's white, thin legs climb the steps behind her until they both disappeared at the top.

A little while later, my mother called down to say lunch was ready, and in that same moment, my father got up to swim. My mother always said he did it on purpose to make us wait for him—especially at dinnertime, after his two bourbon highballs, heading into the powder room to wash his hands and face slowly right as my mother put the hot plates on the table. After so many years, she no longer said anything.

"Are you coming in, son?" he asked.

He walked past me to sit on the stairs and put on his lake sneakers.

"There isn't enough time," I said. "Lunch is ready."

He moved slowly toward the water as if he didn't hear me, stepping unsteadily through the low waves. At one point he teetered over into the water, catching himself with his hand on the rocks below.

I moved my towel into the sun, lay on my back, and stared into the thick, bright sky. A moment later, I heard my sister call annoyingly from the top of the stairs, "You'd better come up for lunch!"

In a few weeks, she would be going away to college, and then I would be alone with Mother and Father.

Her voice went away, and I closed my eyes against the sunlight until the fiery shapes began. So I only half-heard my father's lake call—"Ahhwoooooooah!"—from beyond the pretend darkness, like inside a dream with time passing unseen.

When I opened my eyes, he was standing over me, dripping, toweling off in his over-careful way that embarrassed my mother. "He dries off so meticulously," she said, "as if he was in the bathroom and just gotten out of the shower. But this is a public beach."

His hair was slicked back, and his skin prickly from the cold water. And there was a slight smile across his thin lips, as if he'd discovered something out in the lake and wasn't going to tell.

"C'mon, son. We better go."

I didn't move right away, because I knew he still had to sit on the steps to take off his lake shoes. When he finished, he stood up and poked his toes at Vicki, who was lying in the shade under the beach stairs. She would dig down to the damp sand and then spread out on her belly.

Vicki was losing her hair in places, so you could see the bumpy, slightly blue dog-skin underneath. And she had some kind of rotting stuff around her eyes that made her look even sadder when she stared at you. I always felt bad, because no one paid Vicki much attention. And the dog never liked me. My mother said it was because I was born right after they got her, so Vicki was jealous. My brother said the only reason they got the dog was because they didn't think they were going to have any more children.

My mother was the one who fed her, calling her "the Hund"—German for dog—rather than using her real name. And so Vicki followed my mother around, which is why it was strange she was still lying under the stairs. But Vicki was old, so maybe she had fallen asleep and didn't notice my mother leaving the beach.

My father poked at her again, and she began to get up slowly. Then he lost his balance somehow and started tilting backwards. I figured he would catch himself by grabbing the railing, but he missed, and both his arms started reeling in circles as he tried to save himself. I jumped up, but couldn't get to him in time, so I had to watch as he gave up entirely and let his body drop on the shadow sand behind the stairs, as if he had decided just to sit down hard without using hands.

Vicki was still in her spot, staring as if nothing had happened, even after my father let out a groan like he had maybe broken his back. I tried pulling him up by the hand, but he felt so heavy and kept howling so loud it scared me. I looked around the beach, but there was nobody to help.

Eventually, he moved to his knees, and then slowly stood, still bent over, and stagger-stepped toward the railing. That's when I saw the blood on the gray sand next to an old pipe that stuck out under the staircase two inches above ground. I had never noticed the pipe before.

He put his arm on my shoulder, looked back at the pipe and the blood, and then winced in quiet pain and moved toward the stairs. He moaned once more as he took the first step.

"I can make it myself," he said, pausing on the second stair.

"I'll stay behind, just in case."

I placed my hand on his back, which still felt damp from his swim, and we continued on. Vicki was at my feet the whole time. She must have suddenly realized my mother was gone and was panicking to get to her, unable to pass because we were moving so slowly. But I didn't want her to pass, because my father's accident was partly her fault. I considered kicking at her to keep her back. But I didn't.

My father's ascent seemed to take forever, and I tried to look everywhere except at the back of his bathing suit because I didn't want to see the blood. But when it seemed like I couldn't avoid it, I looked, and was surprised that the blood wasn't very red after all. Maybe it had blended in with his purple bathing suit. But there was bright red trickling down the backs of his legs in zigzag patterns around the fine black hairs, the blood almost the same color as Aunt Frankie's lipstick.

I wished my older sister were at the cottage, because she was a nurse and knew what to do when someone accidentally sits on an old metal pipe. My father was always comfortable with her, calling her "princess," which she hated. But she was still working in Pittsburgh, and wasn't coming to Lake Erie until the second week. My brother could have helped, since he was a medical student, but I knew he would already be back at Gail Pagalis's house.

Halfway up, my father stopped again, and that's when Vicki took her chance to dart past us. She moved pretty well for an old dog, but it still bothered me that she couldn't wait. She barked one time from the top of the stairs to let us know she had gotten there first, then ducked her head and disappeared.

"Twenty-two years . . ." my father mumbled, his head hanging down close to the rail, his breathing heavy in the warm air. "Twenty-two years we've been coming here. Since the war . . . and I never saw that goddamn pipe."

He started moving again, his knees creaking as they often did, his feet looking like slabs of white rubber bending on the wooden steps.

My father is hurt bad, I thought. *He's bleeding from his bum. But he's not even crying.*

At the back door, he paused to dip his feet into an oval pail of water my mother placed there so we wouldn't track sand into the cottage. He dipped his right foot first, leaning his hand against the cottage for balance. And I thought that, this one time, he really should have skipped it. But someone always yelled out, "Don't forget to dunk your feet!"

The blood trickle had reached the back of his knees, but it didn't seem to bother him. He switched to drop his left foot into the speckled pail, disturbing the thin layer of sand at the bottom. I stayed close in case he lost his balance, and I could feel everyone staring at us from the porch right through the screen and hot stillness. Any moment my sister or mother would say, "We started eating without you."

When they took my father to the hospital in Geneva, I had to stay behind to keep Aunt Frankie company. But for some reason, I didn't want to be alone with her. I was good at talking with adults, but Aunt Frankie was the kind of person you were better off looking at rather than talking to.

When she headed back to the beach, I didn't join her. I listened for the screen door to slam, then went up to the bedroom I shared with my brother—my sisters and Aunt Frankie slept on the other side of the wall—just in time to see Aunt Frankie's orange bathing suit disappear down the beach stairs, as if her body wasn't even part of it. I continued to keep watch for a while to make sure she didn't come back up, and then I lay on my bed.

I could smell the strong lake water coming through the windows and stared at the cracks between the faded green wallboards. You could see through to the other bedroom if you got your face close enough. My mother said, "That's the way it is at lake cottages, but you still have to respect everyone's privacy," which was hard to do at Green Gables.

I didn't think I could fall asleep because the air was so heavy and warm, but I wasn't sure what else to do. And I kept seeing Aunt Frankie in my mind's eye, looking around the beach and wondering where I was, smoking her lipstick cigarettes right into the gray sand.

I tried not to think about my mother, who would be disappointed because I hadn't done the right thing in not keeping Aunt Frankie company. And I tried not to think about what they were doing to my father. Because how do you fix a man who is bleeding from the bum?

When the screen door slammed again, I knew Aunt Frankie was back in the cottage and that I must have dozed off. Through the cracks in the floor, I heard the refrigerator door open and the milk bottles rattle on the shelf, and then the sound of a beer can opening. I remained still, not wanting her to hear the bed creak and know where I was.

But I was remembering the time a bee went inside her beer can at the beach, and when she drank it the bee stung her tongue. I couldn't laugh, though, because then the bed would shake.

She didn't head back to the beach like I thought she would. *Maybe she's waiting for me*, I thought.

So I went downstairs. But when I passed the front door, I suddenly turned and went outside, pretending I didn't even know Aunt

Frankie was in the cottage, and made my way light-footed across the brown pine needles and onto the street.

My escape felt good, except that I was hungry because I'd never eaten lunch. *If only I had grabbed something from the kitchen*, I thought. But that would have meant seeing Aunt Frankie. And maybe I deserved the hunger.

I followed the narrow road along the lake bluff, hoping I might run into my brother coming back from the Pagalises. Because he didn't know what had happened to our father.

I passed the house where Ginny Simmons lived. She was an old bridge-playing friend of my mother whom my father said was half-crazy, and remembered the time my mother went through the back door to visit Ginny Simmons, and then left later by way of the front door. Vicki waited at Ginny Simmons's back door for my mother to come out until it grew dark and we were looking all over Madison for her. Around eleven o'clock, Ginny Simmons called and said she had tripped over Vicki while taking out the garbage before bed.

Wee Four cottage, where the priests lived, came up on my right. Father John stood on the porch in his bathing suit, holding a beer in one hand and a cigar in the other. It was too late to avoid him.

"Hello, there!" he called, waving with his thick cigar hand.

"Hello," I said.

I continued walking, which I knew was wrong to do.

"How's your family?" he hollered. "Is your dad up here with you? We were thinking of visiting tonight after dinner."

Wee Four was owned by four priests: Father John Lettau, with the red face and cigars; Father Dave, his younger brother, whom my sister thought was cute; Father Jim Cavanaugh, a large man with glasses who owned a speedboat that went faster than the Pagalises'; and a fourth priest who was never around.

I stopped and turned. "Tonight's not a good night. My father went to the hospital because he sat on a pipe."

Father John paused, as if he wasn't sure what to say. After a few moments, he finally said, "Is he OK?"

"Probably."

"Tell him we'll say a prayer for him."

"OK . . . Maybe you can visit tomorrow."

ᚧᚭᚧᚭᚧ

In the late afternoon, my father returned to Green Gables and, as if nothing unusual had happened, served his bourbon highball and drinks for my mother and Aunt Frankie on the tree stump at the beach. He never mentioned what they did to him at the hospital, but I heard from my sister that he wasn't supposed to go into the water for three days, probably because he had stitches.

After my mother and Aunt Frankie went up to the cottage to start dinner, he reached for his lake shoes.

"Do you want to take an evening dip with me, son?" he asked.

"You're not supposed to go in," I said.

He smiled close-lipped and moved to the stairs to put on his shoes. A few minutes later, he stood up warily, using the railing for support, and then slowly made his way toward the lake.

He's actually going into the polluted water, I thought, *with stitches in his bum.*

I got up and followed him into the low-breaking waves. He stopped when the water was just up to his knees, as if he might be waiting for me to catch up.

"You don't have to swim," I said, almost whispering even though there was no one around.

"It's OK, son," he said, his legs starting to move forward again.

"We can pretend you did," I said.

He stood still but didn't turn around. I put my hand on the round of his shoulder, and we remained like that long enough to notice the fog gathering on the surface of the blackening water and a flock of birds flying overhead in a V-shape, like they always did just before dark. I watched them until they were tiny crosses disappearing into the fading gray-pink sunset.

When my father finally spoke, his two words seemed to circle around the lake and then come back to me from behind: "OK, son."

He turned and, in an unsteady manner, made his way past me toward the shore, his head drooping as if he was looking where to step even though it was too dark to see through the water. I tried to keep up with him, but my foot landed on the side of a slimy rock and I fell sideways into the chilly water.

My father kept moving until he reached the shore. He stopped but didn't turn around.

"At least your mother won't be angry at me," he said, his voice seeming to circle around again.

Then I lost him in the falling darkness as he walked toward the stairs.

The next night, he did take his late evening dip, with the stitches still in his bum, and I sat on the porch and didn't try to stop him. My mother watched through the kitchen window as he came back up the stairs and dunked his feet in the water pail. She was opening a can of Rival dog food for Vicki that I could smell from the porch. Vicki would only eat half of it, and my mother would cover the rest with foil and put it in the refrigerator.

"The next time you get hurt, you take yourself to the hospital," she said to him through the screen.

He ignored her and finished dunking his feet, then headed toward the bathroom.

At dinner, Aunt Frankie talked, whether anyone was listening or not. And my mother kept asking her questions to keep things going.

And when it got dark, the priests came to visit, sitting in chairs at the top of the bluff, smoking cigars and singing songs with my father, who concentrated with closed eyes that I could see whenever he puffed his cigar and the orange sparks lit up the side of his face. Sometimes, a vague smile crossed his lips, and I remembered my oldest brother saying, "The only time Dad is happy is when he is singing"—like at Lake Erie with the priests from Wee Four, my father's belly lifting as he breathed in, his face fading away as his cigar hand dropped to his side.

My sister was sitting there, too, because she wanted to stare at Father Dave through the dark. But my father hardly looked at Father Dave because of the summer before, when we were standing in the lake water, Father Jim's boat anchored in front of our beach, and Father Dave talking about the soldiers standing in water too, only in the Mekong Delta, even though my mother always said "no politics and no religion," especially at Sunday dinner when a priest was always there.

The soldiers are just trying to make their way through that nightmare place of our own making, Father Dave said. And we have to ask ourselves-, My God, what are we doing there?

And this is how the war ruins everything, even when you're just standing with the priests, in the dying lake water on a hot still day, trying not to feel the bottom with your feet.

Inside the lake quiet, my father asked Father Dave if he was a communist and Father Dave didn't answer, standing calm with his dark hair and "movie star looks," as my mother put it, with the faint smell of gasoline from Father Jim's boat mixing in with the dusty lake water, and moving our arms back and forth across the water because of the little black bugs, except for Father John, who held his beer in the air, because no one enjoys his beer like Father John, my mother says, and there is nothing like a cold bottle in God's paradise, he says, drinking naked from the waste up . . . reminding me of the men swimming naked at the Pittsburgh Athletic Club pool when I'd walk to the locker room after judo class, trying not to seem like I was afraid to look at them. Because my mother thought a judo class would be a good thing for a twelve-year-old boy even if she had to drive me all the way to Oakland. The misty air mixing with the warm chlorine dampness, three or four of them bobbing inside the cavern where it is hard to breathe because the roof is too low . . . their white bodies tilting out of the fake blue because it was Men's Swim Time, no ladies allowed, so no sense wearing a bathing suit. "The men do that inside all the athletic clubs," my mother said. "And your father used to swim like that, performing his laps religiously." But I never saw him do that. "And it might be nice for you to take a swim after judo class," she said. But I never did, blaming it on the chlorine smell that bothered my eyes . . .

When I got home afterward, I had to face my weekend chore—emptying the ashes out of the basement incinerator because my father had burned all the paper trash the night before, making the wall feel so hot our house could catch fire like dead sticks with ashes spilling upward into noses because there was no clean way out of it. And adding water to the oily yellow pan outside the ancient furnace that big Mori's dad never fixed right.

And the day before Lake Erie, having to go into the pitch dark cubby-hole off the third-floor bedroom, where all the spiders lived in the attic heat, to get the suitcases. Trying to get out quick as I could, walking on the two-by-sixes so I wouldn't fall through the soft floor, and fearing someone would come up from behind and close the miniature door, leaving me there forever in the cubby-hole darkness where no one can hear you from the other side . . .

The priests sang "Too-Ra-Loo-Ra-Loo-Ra" and "Home on the Range" and "Bicycle Built for Two" and "I've Been Working on the Railroad." And always last—"Mamie Reilly"—while my mother drank her nightly beer on the porch with Aunt Frankie smoking her lipstick cigarettes unseen, except for the moving orange glow.

And how hard it would be on my father, I thought, if my sister was right and we never came back to Lake Erie because the water really was too polluted. And he would have to say goodbye for the last time, harder than all the other goodbye years . . .

. . . when he would leave us in the hot car just as we were packed and ready to go . . . sweating, waiting for the air to move through the open windows, and we couldn't blow the horn because my mother hated that, even if we have to wait for a week, she said, while he walked slowly around Green Gables, already forgetting us, to stand on the bluff and say his secret words through closed lips . . . with no one allowed to get out of the car and walk around to see what he was doing, because no one can ever really watch my father, or know how everything drops away for him, even the lake itself, until he is standing alone and the nothingness around the bluff takes over, and he can't leave . . .

The shadows shifted as my father began the last verse:

Slide Kelly slide,
Casey's at the bat,
Oh, Mamie Reilly, where'd you get that hat?
Down in old Kentucky, old black Joe.
Oh, Mamie, Mamie, Mamie, Mamie Reilly. Hey!

"Hot damn!" my father exclaimed.
And the night went silent.

. . . and the Hill

By the fourth week of September, we all knew to avoid Jackoby in the morning. We had all seen what happened to the red-headed kid, Michael Nicely, on the first day.

We were sitting at the long table in the cafeteria after the buses had dropped us off, and Don Jackoby came by and tugged on Michael Nicely's collar. We thought he had chosen randomly, but Jackoby said, "C'mon, Nicely. You're just the kid I need."

Don Jackoby was a freshman like us, but for some reason he could do whatever he wanted. Maybe because he was a linebacker, or maybe because he could get that crazy look across his eyes that said, "I can do anything, anytime, to any of you."

On that first day of high school, Michael Nicely went along willingly. And since the bell hadn't rung yet, we walked behind them and watched as Jackoby placed Nicely inside the freight elevator in the back of the building next to the kitchen. He swung the elevator door down and fixed it so Nicely wouldn't be able to open it. It seemed like he had done this before—as if it was almost a chore.

One of Jackoby's friends went upstairs to jam the button so the elevator wouldn't stop once it reached the second floor. Instead, it would automatically come back down, and then go back up again, and then down again, never stopping.

Whenever the elevator reappeared, we could see Michael Nicely's face through the little square of glass in the elevator door. His eyes were wide open, but he wasn't crying or screaming. He just looked as if he was wondering how long the ride was going to last.

Don Jackoby smiled every time Nicely's face reappeared in the elevator window, as if he was admiring his work. He even waved to him, but Michael Nicely didn't wave back.

When the bell rang, we left to find our homerooms, with Michael Nicely still going up and down. Later, some kid on his way to the bathroom said he heard Nicely screaming, his voice echoing down the long hallway. But all the doors were closed, so no one else could hear him.

In homeroom, Brother Ed Zileski explained what it was going to be like at South Hills Catholic High School for Boys. But for some of us, South Catholic already meant Don Jackoby and the elevator, and who would be next. So every morning I sat far away from Jackoby and hoped he wouldn't look at me as he made his way around the table. After school, I left as fast as I could to catch the bus home.

Don Jackoby had his own club of boys called Loafers Incorporated. In order to earn your way into the club and become a "loafing buddy," you had to spend a certain number of "loafing hours" with Jackoby. They mostly loafed in the evenings at the circle at Mount Lebanon Park. I saw them down there a couple times, but I never liked loafing in the park.

Sometimes a senior named Mac, short for McHenry, showed up after school in a yellow Chrysler and asked kids who lived in Mt. Lebanon if they wanted a ride home. I always said no, except for one day in late September when the bus hadn't arrived and I saw Jackoby heading my way down the sidewalk with two other loafers, Piggy Curlan and Joe Guff.

Mac was seventeen or eighteen, but he looked like he was thirty. His head was too big for his short body, and he brushed his brown hair straight back like adults do. He drove his car slowly on purpose because it gave him more time to talk, which he also did slowly, his words sounding as though he wanted to be your friend, which didn't feel right, his head rolling toward you with bulgy eyes staring instead of watching the road. When I got out of the car, I said "thanks for helping me out this one time."

The next day Scott Payton came up to me at the start of Brother Don Herr's math class. He was a short kid with blond hair combed down his forehead and looked like he wasn't old enough to be in high school, which is why some kids made fun of him. For some reason, though, Don Jackoby protected him. *Paytee-cake, Paytee-cake, Jackoby's boy*, the kids sang when Jackoby wasn't around.

"You rode home with Mac the faggot yesterday," he said, standing close to my desk to look tough. "I saw you. Did he mo you on the way home?"

"I only rode with him once. How many times have you ridden with Mac?"

My voice was louder than his, and it brought laughter across the room. Scott Payton's face reddened, as if he was about to explode.

Brother Don told everyone to take their seats, so Scott Payton slumped back to his desk at the front of the row. A few minutes later, though, when Brother Don turned to write some numbers on the board, Scott Payton stood up abruptly and made his way back toward my desk. Within seconds, he was swinging his fists at me, trying to hit my face. But I blocked him because my arms were longer.

"You're the faggot!" he screamed. "You're the faggot!!"

Brother Don Herr came down the aisle so fast his cassock flew out behind him. He pulled Scott Payton by the ear across the front of the room and out the door. The whole time, Scott Payton was trying not to cry.

When Brother Don came back from the principal's office, he returned to the chalkboard. Then he stopped, as if he had changed his mind about something, and walked slowly down the aisle towards me. He stood so close his cassock touched my knees. Tilting down, he stared through his thick glasses, and I could see how perfectly smooth and flat his crew cut was. A moment later, he lifted his head around to address the whole class.

"We will never have a disturbance in my class, gentlemen. Do you understand?"

"Yes," we all said, each of us trying not to see his eyes.

I looked toward the window, hoping this would be the end of it.

"Good . . . Put your hands on your desk," he said, looking down at me. "Hands on desk," he repeated, moving close, his cassock smelling like old laundry.

He slowly folded up his black sleeves, revealing white, hairy arms underneath—his flesh soft-looking, like all brothers must have, I thought, even though we never saw it. They only showed their faces and hands, and sometimes feet, like Brother Michael, who wore sandals because he was from the Philippines.

Brother Don raised his arms high, as if he was going to pray in a showoff way, then held them there, above his head, for a slant of seconds . . . *like the man who plays cymbals in the Pittsburgh Symphony my mother took me to one time, getting the timing right with the conductor's signals, and then the rush of air like music you can feel before hearing . . . and the smacking is like air, too, from red hands like priests' have, through ears that are meant for music, my Uncle Ted says . . .*

The rushing air hurt more than the darkening sting that followed, turning my eyes into burning water because sound travels slower than touching, mathematics explaining everything, Brother Don told us. But my ears were too close for the clapping of two hands with all his might, pushing me down into a darkness where thinking doesn't exist, like when Marla Hawkins hugged my chest real hard and I had to remember where I was. My head rolled like it was somebody else's head, because the neck is weak. I tried to climb back out of it to where I was before, but that is hard to do after your ears are boxed, like stunning an animal, someone said, delivered from Brother Don's eyes without expression. "I didn't do anything. Scott Payton did," I wanted to say, but my lips were numb and Brother Don Herr was already making his way back up the aisle while another wave of pain pierced like darts, making me think I should just throw up, with the tears coming on that I didn't want, because Scott Payton might find out and tell everyone.

Brother Don's cassock fluttered behind him like a black curtain moving across a stage. When he reached the chalkboard, he started writing numbers again, stopping for a moment to look back at us.

"If anyone disturbs my class, they will get the same thing. Is that clear, gentlemen?"

Everyone nodded yes, except me, because I already knew.

"Good. Now copy down these integers."

We all started writing quietly, but my hand shook so much the numbers weren't clear, which was strange since it was my ears that had been boxed. And I wanted to touch them more than anything, to stop the hot ringing. But Brother Don said "hands on the desk," and the burning water in my eyes kept on . . .

I lowered my head so no one could see. I wasn't crying. I just couldn't stop, which is different.

ᚹᚲᚨᚹᚲᚨ

After lunch, on the smoking patio outside the cafeteria, some of the kids talked about "Mac the faggot," as if it had become official. So I didn't expect his car to appear at the drive-up after school. And I had become the kid who got his ears boxed, and Scott Payton the kid who got mo'd by Mac. And that's probably why no one saw Scott

Payton the rest of the day.

Mac's brother, Conor, who was a sophomore, said he would beat up the first kid he saw after school who was a faggot. Conor played hockey and had little scars on his eyebrows and forehead. So I watched out for him, and for Jackoby, after the last bell rang, waiting for the bus inside the gymnasium doors where no one could see me. But when a group of kids ran by heading toward the parking lot, I had to follow.

By the first row of cars, Joe Schetzke was down on the pavement, jerking around and screaming, "Fuck you, McHenry!"

And Conor McHenry yelled back through the open window of his red Camaro, "Fuck you, Schetzke, you faggot," which was strange, because no one thought Schetzke was a faggot. Unless maybe it didn't matter to Conor McHenry.

Mr. Palmary, the principal, showed up. He was also the football coach, and a really big man who always winced like he had pain in his face. He told Joe Schetzke an ambulance would come to take him to the hospital. Then he seemed to forget about Schetzke and talked to Conor McHenry, who was still in his car.

"Some of the students say you were speeding out of the parking lot, Mr. McHenry. Is this correct? And that you opened your car door on purpose right into Mr. Schetzke's leg. What's the matter with you, son? You broke his leg."

Conor got out of his car slowly. When he stood, he was nearly as tall as Mr. Palmary. Everything felt calm in that moment, except for Schetzke still screaming, "Fuck you, McHenry!"

"Stop saying that word, Mr. Schetzke, or I will suspend you for use of language," Mr. Palmary said. "The ambulance will be here any minute. You'll be fine, son."

But Joe Schetzke kept right on screaming, "Fuck you, McHenry!" And we knew he wasn't going to stop until the ambulance took him away, no matter what the principal said.

"Mr. Palmary, I thought he was a mailbox," Conor McHenry finally answered.

"What?"

"I shouldn't have been speeding, sir."

"Why would you open your car door?"

"I needed to mail some letters, and thought he was a mailbox. I didn't stop in time, sir. And didn't see it was Schetzke until—"

"Where are the letters?"

"I don't know. I must have forgotten them. I thought he was a mailbox, sir. I didn't see him."

Some kid in the crowd asked, "Why did he run over Schetzke if Schetzke isn't a faggot?"

"Because he thought he was a mailbox, you idiot," someone answered.

"No, he doesn't like Schetzke's mother," someone else said. "Remember, he mooned her last week?"

But I remembered that it was two other kids who mooned Mrs. Schetzke at Mitchell's Corner, not Conor McHenry. Mrs. Schetzke got the license plate number and Mr. Palmary suspended them. When Jackoby found out, he told his loafing buddies, "This will be the beginning of a new tradition: mooning Mrs. Schetzke!"

Jackoby had other games, like chewing gum at the South Hills Village mall and spitting it on the floor to see who would step on it. "If a nigger with a hat steps on it," Jackoby said, "you automatically win."

Bill Milner, whom Jackoby hated because he was such a cake-eater, liked to repeat the phrase "nigger with a hat," because he thought it would make Jackoby like him. But instead, Jackoby threw rocks at him. One time, he did it during all of recess, the rocks bouncing off Bill Milner's chest while he just stood there pretending they didn't hurt, with water in his eyes and never moving an inch.

Mr. Palmary told everyone to go home. But I didn't know what to do because I had already missed my bus. So I headed back toward the gymnasium. Then I changed my mind and decided to walk home, which I had never done before because it was over five miles with lots of steep hills.

I noticed Craig McCann in the parking lot getting into his Cutlass Supreme. "Old Blue," he called it. And I asked him for a ride.

"I have to help Brother Michael with a lab project," he said. "I'm just getting stuff out of my car. I couldn't give you a ride anyway, since I only have my permit."

"OK," I said, and continued on.

Up ahead, Mr. Tillman, the English teacher, was getting into his orange VW. I wanted to say something but didn't really know him, except that his mother was sister to Ginny Simmons who lived up at Lake Erie. He looked like a skinnier version of John Lennon, with his long, curly hair, wire-rim glasses, and mustache. And everyone knew he was only teaching at South Catholic to avoid the draft, because they weren't taking teachers away to Vietnam.

My mother told me Bill Tillman graduated first in his class at Notre Dame, but turned down a Ph.D. scholarship to Yale because they had begun drafting graduate students and he was against the war. I wished I could talk to him about it, but Mr. Tillman was already driving past, lighting a cigarette and opening his car window at the same time.

The ambulance drove by me without the siren on and the back door open, so I could hear Joe Schetzke still screaming, "Fuck you, McHenry!" The ambulance made a sharp turn and headed down the exit drive, and eventually I couldn't hear him anymore.

When I reached the end of the parking lot, I noticed some football players gathered at the top of the cross-country hill, fooling around with a metal garbage can someone must have dragged up there. I left the road and walked toward the lower field, where a group of kids were hanging out.

"What's going on?" I asked.

"Taddy Keegan's going to roll down the hill in that garbage can," someone said. "It was his idea."

I could see Taddy Keegan climbing into the silvery can and giving directions about how to put the lid on. His hair was longer and over his eyes. He looked like someone I had never known.

A moment later, the football players turned the can on its side and rolled it toward the brink of the hill.

"Give it a good push!" a voice yelled up the hill.

It was Billy Creely, standing by himself with an excited look in his eyes, as if he couldn't wait for Taddy Keegan to do the roly-poly down the weedy, brown cross-country hill. But it made me feel sick, *like when Coach Pitchke made us run up and down the hill in the late summer heat a few weeks earlier, right after we got back from Lake Erie. I only signed up for cross country because my brother had done it ten years earlier, and Coach Harry Pitchke was his old teammate. And my brother was always talking about the time he got spiked across the belly when he fell one day and someone stepped on him, lifting his shirt to show us at the dinner table, my mother telling him to stop because we always had to keep our shirts on at dinner even if it was really hot and you had spike marks. Which made me want to fall down and get spiked, too, so Harry Pitchke wouldn't have to tell me not to worry about throwing up before the races, because everyone does that sometimes, he said.*

Like at the Labor Day race at Schenley Park, when I nearly had the lead just before the top of Heartbreak Hill, with the bowl-shaped park below and my head tilting with the vomit, watching the other kids' feet pass upside-down in a race measured from the moon by someone who never threw up, deciding right then I wouldn't do it anymore but trying to catch up anyway . . . into the thinning trees on the downhill side, viewing the city in the distance and the Cathedral of Learning protruding into the soft cloudy sky, and then into thicker trees near the Pitts-

burgh Conservatory, where my mother always took us to see the flower show at Christmas, my sister loving the warm damp-green smell, then faster along the level path next to a wooden fence with Schenley Park Road on the other side, where cars would stop and watch us running without water, because you're never allowed to drink until the end, my body tilting forward too much and my arms losing rhythm against my sides in a way that Coach Pitchke didn't like.

And then the one voice I never expected coming from the blur of faces near the end of the fence--"OK, son," and seeing his businessman's hat, but still not sure it was him, nearly tripping on some stick in the pathway to see his face and one of his suit jacket elbows hanging over the fencepost, his eyes lit up behind the black-framed glasses for only a second, the only time my father ever came to watch me do anything—but it didn't matter, because I was quitting. My mother just didn't know it yet. And she would say it was OK, as long as I finished the season—the sooner the better for my father, because then he would have one less thing to worry about not doing . . .

The garbage can rolled slowly at first, even though the hill was pretty steep. Then it veered off-course into the taller weeds and picked up speed, the lid staying on because Taddy Keegan was probably holding it from the inside.

The boys at the bottom ran to catch up and missed seeing the can hit a rock hidden behind the tall grass, popping the lid off, but Taddy Keegan stayed inside with his head sticking out just a little. His face hit another rock and then the can turned in slower circles until it came to rest on a patch of dried mud in the lower field.

When he stood up, we could see the blood on his cheek and down his arm where he had been cut by the edge of the can. He was laughing, though, his eyes half open, not looking at anyone, and his neck vibrating as if he were trying to shake something from the top of his body.

Everyone waited for him to stop laughing. And he finally did, as he bent to examine the dented can like he was going to fix it some-how. A minute later, he spoke in a TV voice that I knew wasn't the real Taddy Keegan. But maybe there never was a real Taddy Keegan.

"Let's do it again, boys. I know I can make it all the way. If you'll just kindly carry the can back up the hill."

He wiped the blood from his face with his hand, then rubbed his hand on the back of his pants. A football player picked up the can, and they headed up the hill together, walking diagonally through the weeds, reminding me of how we used to climb through the crown vetch up Kaufman's Hill.

I wanted to say something to him, but a horn tooted and I turned back to see McCann in Old Blue at the bend in the road wav-ing for me.

Taddy Keegan was almost to the top of the hill, his body leaning into it, his legs invisible in the high grass.

"Taddy!" I yelled. "Taddy!"

He turned around but didn't seem to recognize me.

McCann tooted again, his car moving slowly as if he wasn't go-ing to wait. When I turned back, Taddy Keegan had reached the top of the hill. And then I ran . . .

"Do you want a ride?" McCann yelled as I got closer.

"I thought you only had a permit?"

"So what?" he said, jerking his head a little and pushing his glasses back up his nose. "No one's going to notice if you jump in now."

At the top of the cross-country hill, Taddy Keegan was stepping inside his silvery can. But I didn't want to see him get bloody any-more just so everyone else could say how crazy he was.

McCann turned the car around with one hand. "Don't you just love power steering?" he said as we started down the school drive-way.

Through the rear window, I could see the garbage can beginning to roll. Eventually, the steep road got in the way and I couldn't see it anymore.

In the summer, I had sometimes gone up to Craig McCann's house after our dinner, and his parents would still be having their cocktails in the living room. They'd direct me to the kitchen, where Craig would pull a steak from the broiler and a baked potato out of the toaster oven. I was surprised he could cook dinner all by himself.

I sat with him while he ate, neither of us saying much. And afterwards, we'd go upstairs to a little closet room where he had a ham radio, and he'd talk to people on the dial, some close by and some in another country. McCann sounded like an adult, and the people he talked to didn't know the difference.

He also had a transistor radio he built himself and some homemade musical instruments, like a gut bucket made from an old laundry tub with a string attached to a broom handle that he played with his eyes closed as if he knew what he was doing.

When I left, his parents would still be sitting with their drinks in the living room, only his mother had changed into her nightgown. She'd wave goodbye from her chair, and I wondered just how long they would wait before having their dinner.

And maybe that's why McCann seemed older than other kids, and why he drove his Cutlass with his arm out the window, smoking a Pall Mall unfiltered cigarette.

"Did you see Taddy Keegan go down the hill?" I asked.

"You should have heard him at lunch," he said. "Taddy was betting everyone he could roll down the hill without falling out of the can. He seemed to care about it more than they did."

We passed Jonny Logan walking home alone, just as I'd planned to do. *It's too bad Jonny Logan's not at the lower field*, I thought, *be-*

cause he would like seeing Taddy Keegan roll down the hill.

In grade school, Jonny Logan kept asking Taddy to fight him, and Taddy Keegan kept saying no because Jonny Logan was too small . . . *until our last day of school at St. Thomas Moore, and Jonny Logan wouldn't let it go, so Taddy Keegan beat him up at lunchtime on the front lawn of the convent underneath a light falling rain . . . We all stood on the soggy grass watching Jonny Logan move in circles with Taddy at the center, punching into Jonny Logan's cheeks, over and over again, each time making that "perfect smacking sound" that felt sickening, with Taddy asking, "Do you give up?" and Jonny Logan shaking his head, and Taddy punching him again, and Jonny Logan's head snapping back again after the smacking sound, his fists never getting close to Taddy but still moving his useless arms and dancing in circles and not falling down, because Jonny Logan didn't care how many times he got hit . . . until a nun ran out from the convent into the gray drizzle and made us all walk away, Taddy Keegan too, with Jonny Logan still standing there under the rain, yelling to Taddy, "C'mon, I haven't given up yet. I haven't given up . . ."*

McCann reached for an eight-track tape on the front seat between us.

"Listen to this," he said. "The Moody Blues made an album with the fucking London Symphony!"

"Aren't you worried about Taddy?" I asked.

"He'll be OK. He always is. But Conor McHenry, they'll send him to public school at Keystone Oaks, where they send all the kids who get expelled."

Like Barry Duquesne, I thought, who got transferred after his first week at South Catholic because he lit his neighbor's cat on fire after dipping it in gasoline, the owner coming out just in time to see his cat screeching in flames down the dark street. One time when I saw Barry Duquesne sledding at Spalding Circle, he wanted to show me some magazines he kept inside a hollow tree, but I never went with him.

The music began, one of the Moody Blues talking more than singing, something about being alone at night and a man waking up his steeds to warm the countryside.

"Where are we going?" I asked.

"We're going for a drive. You ever been out Route 519? Don't worry, we'll be back by dinner."

I wasn't sure if he meant his dinnertime or mine.

After you learn to drive, you can go anywhere you want, I thought, and figure how to get there on your own. You just have to find your way home.

We passed South Park, where my brother used to harness-race ostriches at the summer fair. And after that, I didn't recognize anything. But I knew we weren't in Pittsburgh anymore. Yet it wasn't the suburbs or countryside, either, but something in-between . . .

McCann talked about a new modular system the high school was switching to in January.

"It will be like college," he said. "We can leave school and drive somewhere for breakfast and no one will know."

I noticed a sign saying we had entered the town of Library, Pennsylvania. Some black kids were walking down the sidewalk, which surprised me, because I thought all the black people lived in the Hill District.

"Have you heard about the shack?" McCann asked, turning his face toward me. "Tyson and Dunlow built it with old pieces of wood from their garages."

"What is it?"

"It's a place where no one can bother you. Like having your own little house. It's in the woods beyond their dead end. Only a few kids know about it."

The eight-track player started making a squeaking noise right in the middle of the Moody Blues singing about Tuesday afternoon. So

McCann pulled the tape out.

"This tape's fucked up," he said.

He twitched around a little, as if trying to get comfortable in his seat. Then he reached under his legs for another eight-track on the floor that said "King Crimson."

"Smythe is bringing some marijuana to the shack on Friday and we're going to try it," he said.

And I'll have to tell my mother I'm going someplace else, I thought. And I usually don't tell her anything, so I never have to lie. It could be like smoking tobies with Taddy Keegan up on Kaufman's hill . . . He lit the toby for me and we sat there smoking, and we didn't even have to talk to each other . . . And on the day he lost his white rat that lived on top of his head, because Kenny Franz threw the bat into Billy Creely's eye . . . I told Taddy I would help him look for the rat even though it was getting dark, but he didn't want me to . . .

I could still see Taddy Keegan sitting on his white rock, but I couldn't see myself. Because you can never really see yourself when you remember the past. And that's why you never really know what happened to you, or what you looked like. And you can't recognize yourself on a tape recorder, either, because we get carried away from ourselves so easily, until Kaufman's Hill looks much smaller than it used to be. And beyond . . . the new woods Taddy Keegan told me about that I really did explore one time, and the tree fort was there, just like Taddy Keegan said. But there was no way up to it, unless you could somehow climb a tree that had no lower branches. So I wondered how anyone built it there, high among the pointed leaves flickering green and silver. And it was too late to go back there again, because an old-age home and a chain restaurant were sitting in its place.

A horseshoe-shaped sign said Route 519. *McCann knows where he's going after all,* I thought. *Like getting lost and you don't have to worry because someone else knows how to find the way.*

"The Court of the Crimson King" sounded pretty good. The words felt important, so I tried to memorize them. But they kept getting away while the music stayed around longer, making it hard to pay attention to anything else. I wanted to see the "slowly turning grinding wheel" and "the rusted chains of the prison moons," even though I didn't know what they were.

"We're in Canonsburg now," McCann said. "Look, there's the lake."

I could see the causeway leading across to Canonsburg Lake, where Paddy Keegan drove us one time in Mrs. Keegan's blue station wagon on a really hot summer day . . . *with car inner tubes we blew up at the Esso Station . . . floating them around the lake anywhere we wanted—me and Taddy and his brother Timmy and Georgie-Porgie . . . until the fishermen yelled at us for making too much noise. So we paddled over to the causeway and waited for Paddy Keegan to pick us up at four o'clock like he said he would. But we ended up waiting until it was nearly dark, floating the whole time, spinning our inner tubes in circles . . . the water feeling cooler than the thick, warm air, with no one else around except for the fishermen in rowboats we could no longer see . . . and Georgie-Porgie telling us to watch out for fish feeding at dusk that could bite us in the ass, but no one wanted to look afraid or get out of his inner tube . . .*

. . . We finally recognized Mrs. Keegan's car coming across the causeway because it had only one headlight . . . a pididdle, my older sister called it, and we counted how many pididdles we could see driving at night around Lake Erie . . .

. . . On the way home, Paddy seemed more friendly than usual— because he had been drinking for hours, Georgie-Porgie later said, and almost forgot to pick us up.

"The next town is Cecil, PA," McCann announced. "Population 132."

He punched his fingers in the air as if he was proud he knew exactly how many people lived in a place so far away. And I kept thinking about how it was getting dark and he wasn't allowed to drive at night on a learner's permit.

The Crimson King got harder to hear. So I asked McCann if the tape was going bad again. He said no, so I figured the problem must be from what Brother Don did to my ears in the morning. *This is the way it happens*, I thought. And the more you worry about it, the harder it gets to hear, because everything sounds farther away and you can't pull it back on a string.

The road narrowed and became more tree-covered, so there was nothing to see under the expanding shadows until McCann finally stopped at a rundown looking place called the Dew Drop Inn. When he got out of the car, I noticed it was almost completely dark outside, which meant we'd been riding in Old Blue longer than I thought.

The heavy graying light felt different somehow, the air almost green-looking beneath the mist. *The sky is thinking about rain*, my mother liked to say, and my father believed that twilight was the finest time of day. But it can feel different in a strange place, making things you don't know fade away just as you focus on them—the weeping willow tree in front of the Dew Drop Inn and the parked cars, all falling into a gray-green painting you can't touch.

The front door of the inn was hard to see. It seemed to disappear and then come back again, and then disappear once more. But McCann stood solid, his hands in his pockets, walking toward the inn and then turning to face me. In the lost twilight, he looked like Taddy Keegan, only shorter and with glasses . . . *and he would be there on top of Kaufman's Hill . . . and there wouldn't be any Creelys to worry about with their rat-sticks waving . . .*

"C'mon," he said from across the dirt parking lot. "Let's go in. Big Mori said they serve minors if you act older and don't look nervous."

"I'm only fourteen."

"And I'm only fifteen."

A flock of birds flew noisily overhead like they always do the moment night falls, even when you don't know where you are.

He waited a few more seconds, then continued walking toward the front door hidden beneath a low awning. His shape seemed to change in the dim light until he could have been anyone.

"Wait up!" I yelled, opening the car door to make my way toward the Dew Drop Inn.

Acknowledgments

My gratitude to Al Landwehr, Kevin Clark, Mary Kay Harrington, Ginger Adcock, and Lisa Coffman for their early insights and suggestions, especially their encouraging me to trust the perspective and voice of the "boy"; to Rose Pass for her faithful editing of the first draft; to my old friend Howard Zinn, who is out there somewhere, for his soulful belief in this book; to my wife, Patricia, for helping me realize, after my mother died in 2004 (my father had died decades earlier), that it was OK to reveal more deeply the darker presence of the past; and to my fourteen year-old daughter, Maya, who always believed in *Kaufman's Hill* and who will now be allowed to read it.

I am particularly grateful to Todd Pierce for his crucial advice after the manuscript was completed, and to Harrison Demchick, my editor at Bancroft, for his magnificent job editing the manuscript, and to Bruce Bortz, publisher, for his passion and commitment.

Bravo and thanks to artist Tracey Harris for translating my vision for the cover into a spectacular painting, and to Thom Brajkovich, architect, for his ingenious execution of the maps.

I also want to express my appreciation to *The Gettysburg Review* and editor Peter Stitt for publishing Chapter Twelve, "The Rivers," in the Winter 2014 issue.

Finally, I want to say that, although the names have been changed, everything in this book is true as I remember it, especially inside the moments of twilight.

About the Author

John C. Hampsey is the author of *Paranoia and Contentment: A Personal Essay on Western Thought*, the first book to view paranoia in a positive light. Hampsey has published more than thirty stories and essays in such places as *The Gettysburg Review*, *The Midwest Quarterly*, *Antioch Review*, *The Alaska Quarterly*, and *Philosophy and Literature*. Born and raised in Pittsburgh, Pennsylvania, Hampsey now lives in California. He is Professor of Romantic and Classical Literature at Cal Poly, San Luis Obispo, where he has won the University Distinguished Teaching Award.

For more information visit *www.johnchampsey.com*

More Praise for John C. Hampsey's
Kaufman's Hill

"This is what an American childhood used to be like before it was organized out of existence: an anarchic voyage into the unknown realms of human possibility—by turns, violent, uncanny, ridiculous, and radiant. It's a wonderful accomplishment."
—**Robert Inchausti, author of *The Ignorant Perfection of Ordinary People*, *Spitwad Sutras*, and *Thomas Merton's American Prophecy***

"Touches on something about boyhood within the expansiveness of life that I can't remember anyone doing, especially with this voice and perspective."
—**Al Landwehr, Writer of short fiction, And Professor Emeritus of Creative Writing, Cal Poly San Luis Obispo**

"A wonderful, sensitive, and compelling read with a sensibility in both content and style that is simply breath-taking."
—**Cathie Brettschneider, Humanities Editor, University of Virginia Press**

"In a way no one has before, it captures the dynamics of the lost world of boyhood with sensitivity but without sentimentality."
—**Kevin Clark, Author, *Self-Portrait with Expletives***